Day-to-Day Dyslexia in the Classroom

Dyslexia cuts across class, age and intelligence. All schools will have pupils with dyslexia and teachers of children of all ages need to be aware of the teaching methods and approaches which are most effective with these children.

This fully revised and updated edition of a classic text offers invaluable advice to teachers on how they can recognise specific learning difficulties and give practical help to children in their classes. Written in an accessible, jargon-free language, it provides guidelines on the way children with dyslexia learn language and achieve literacy and numeracy skills. It also includes chapters on handwriting, study skills and classroom management, while bearing in mind numerous demands made on classroom teachers.

This new edition includes reference to the National Literacy Strategy, how to make effective use of Teaching Assistants, and includes exercises which enable dyslexic people to become more ready to learn academically, as well as commentary on teaching children with diagnosed dyspraxia and Attention Deficit Disorder.

This is the essential companion to dyslexia that no teacher, student teacher, Special Educational Needs Coordinator or Teaching Assistant can afford to be without.

Joy Pollock is an independent dyslexia consultant. **Elisabeth Waller** was also a dyslexia consultant. **Rody Politt** has taught in both primary and secondary sectors, as well as lecturing and speaking at conferences on dyslexia.

A nine-year-old's dream of escape from school

Day-to-Day Dyslexia in the Classroom

2nd edition

Joy Pollock, Elisabeth Waller
and Rody Politt

 RoutledgeFalmer
Taylor & Francis Group

LONDON AND NEW YORK

First published 1994
Reprinted 1995 (twice), 1996
Revised Edition 1997
Reprinted 1998, 1999, 2002, 2003 (twice)
Second Edition published 2004
by RoutledgeFalmer
2 Park Square, Milton Park, Abingdon, Oxon OX14 4RN

Simultaneously published in the USA and Canada
by RoutledgeFalmer
270 Madison Avenue, New York, NY 10016

Reprinted 2005

RoutledgeFalmer is an imprint of the Taylor & Francis Group

© 2004 Joy Pollock, Elisabeth Waller and Rody Politt

Typeset in Sabon by
Florence Production Ltd, Stoodleigh, Devon

Printed and bound in Great Britain by
TJ International Ltd, Padstow, Cornwall

British Library Cataloguing in Publication Data
A catalogue record for this book is available from
the British Library

Library of Congress Cataloging in Publication Data
Pollock, Joy
    Day-to-day dyslexia in the classroom/Joy Pollock,
    Elisabeth Waller, and Rody Politt – 2nd ed.
        p. cm.
    Includes bibliographical references and index.
    1. Dyslexic children – Education. 2. Dyslexia. I. Waller,
    Elisabeth. II. Politt, Rody. III. Title.
    LC4708.P65 2004
    371.91'44–dc22   2003026277

ISBN 0–415–33971–5 (hbk)
ISBN 0–415–33972–3 (pbk)

To the memory of
JEAN AUGUR
who worked tirelessly for
dyslexic people of all ages
we dedicate this book.

Contents

Foreword

Sadly, Elisabeth Waller died in December 2000. However, Elisabeth did live long enough to know that her project with Joy Pollock was so very well received and regarded by teachers. *Day-to-Day Dyslexia in the Classroom* was written primarily for teachers (though it has been greatly appreciated by parents too) and its success is a mark of Elisabeth and Joy's knowledge of dyslexia and of teaching situations. It is the teacher's understanding of children's learning difficulties that enables them to be empathetic and to engage in appropriate teaching strategies.

In this edition, Rody Politt has collaborated with Joy to expand the content to further address Joy's belief in the concept of teaching the whole child. Over a period of many years, Rody has developed an expertise in the holistic approach to teaching in primary and secondary schools. Information on many well-tried and tested exercises have been included in this edition and they, alongside the cognitive interventions, enable dyslexic children and those with associated learning difficulties to make much more rapid progress in their learning.

In the intervening time between this and the first edition in 1994 there have, not surprisingly, been changes and developments in the dyslexia world. We seem to be moving from that rather clumsy compromise term 'specific learning difficulties/dyslexia' to accepting that there is a cluster of specific learning difficulties of which dyslexia is probably the most common. We have seen the concept of the 'Dyslexia Friendly School' introduced, with one consequence being that more dyslexic pupils are being recognised, creating a greater need for books which offer clear advice for busy teachers.

This edition does just that, once again striking a careful balance between providing good, practical information and being a jargon-free succinct read for busy teachers.

Steve Chinn

Acknowledgements

Our thanks go to Dr Steve Chinn (who kindly wrote the Foreword), Barbara Pheloung, Hilary Cook and many other colleagues, friends and pupils for their support and comments, and Jayne Ruffell Ward for the illustrations in Chapter 5.

Especial thanks go to Lynda Codling for her dedicated work, helpful suggestions and continual good humour while typing the script.

We should also like to thank the following for permission to quote from or reproduce sections of their work in this book: Peter Gilchrist, Ann Henderson, Vicki Burge, Learning Materials Ltd, Oxford University Press and Lynn Wendon and especially Barbara Pheloung.

Authors' note: In order to facilitate reading, teachers are referred to as feminine and pupils as masculine. No discrimination is intended.

Introduction

DISLECKSIA

a bifrent wai ov lerning

Don't miss this page – be sure to read it before Chapter 1!

Dyslexia should be seen as a different learning ability rather than as a disability. It only becomes a disability if it goes unrecognised and the teaching is inappropriate, resulting in the child's failure to gain competence in literacy. A lack of such competence is a real handicap in today's society.

The term dyslexia has been used because it seems to be the most widely used and most apt term. It has been coined from the Greek and literally means **difficulty with** (dys) **words** (lexis). It refers to difficulty with words read, words spelt, words pronounced, words written and association of meanings with words. There are many people who still prefer to use the term 'specific learning disability', which now includes attention deficit disorder (ADD) and dyspraxia, as well as speech and language processing problems.

In most research projects it seems that there is a small group who do not fit neatly into the particular findings. This underlines the danger of dogmatic statements with regard to the nature of dyslexia and emphasises the paramount importance of seeing each pupil as an individual.

This book views dyslexia from an educational standpoint. Dyslexia, be it severe, moderate or mild, cuts across class, age and intelligence, and all schools will have some dyslexic children. An awareness that there are certain teaching methods and practical approaches which are effective with such children is essential for class teachers of both junior and senior schools and, in many instances, may also be of relevance to adult literacy tutors.

Chapters 1 and 14 give the overall picture of dyslexia. The different ways of learning can be found in the other chapters as the specific needs of certain pupils come to mind.

Chapter 1

Dyslexia

This book is primarily for class teachers. However, it includes much information of interest to special needs teachers and parents.

In recent years the number of children with learning difficulties seems to have increased considerably. Some of this might well be due to people's greater awareness of their problems, but there is another consideration that is gaining much credence. This is that of a child's physical development.

It is now recognised that the developmental stages of a child's physical progress – even before birth – are of vital importance to a child's ability to learn in the classroom, thrive in school and, indeed, in life.

It is generally estimated that 20 per cent of pre-school children are not ready to learn, however intelligent they are. Intelligence cannot compensate for maturity. Each successive year puts more demands on growing children. As they develop they have to listen more carefully, look in more detail, sit still for longer, remember more information, do more than one thing at a time, work from left to right ... the list is almost endless. Having the right learning equipment at the right time is essential.

All children are born with a blueprint for development and there is a specific order for each stage. Motor or movement development is shadowed by the development of the sensory system, which also has a specific sequence. First, the sense of balance is developed in the vestibular system (found in the inner ear), and then the sense of touch, followed by auditory and visual senses. If some of the very early stages of development are missed, then children experience problems in later life. The good news is that, as motor and sensory development occurs in us all in exactly the same way, we can retrace our developmental steps to discover at which stage there was a gap and fill it in. Children develop at different speeds and may take a very long time to complete one stage or another but the sequence is always the same.

As the opportunity for exercise has decreased considerably these days, well-proven exercises which enable children – and adults – to be more ready to learn in class have been incorporated in this book (pages 45–51).

These exercises, together with the tuition recommended, will enable all pupils to catch up with their peers at a much quicker pace.

Many children with special educational needs of varying sorts are found in mainstream schools, and the class teacher has to devise teaching strategies to enable them to learn. Their needs have often gone unrecognised and they are thought to be a bit odd; some dyslexic children are considered to be lazy if they are obviously bright orally, but do not come up to the same standard on paper. Those with speech and language processing problems are also to be found in mainstream classes, as indeed are children with attention deficit disorders and dyspraxia. This obviously puts extra responsibility on class teachers.

Whether it is the policy of integration, financial constraints, or lack of recognition of a particular special educational need, there is no doubt that the class teacher these days is faced with being a subject teacher and a specialist in certain learning difficulties all rolled into one. It is unreasonable to expect schoolteachers to know all about medical areas of child developmental care and diseases which are the province of the paediatrician, or the educational problems dealt with by a chartered educational psychologist, or about the processing and understanding of speech which is the field of the speech and language therapist, or the areas of specific difficulties with reading, spelling and numbers which are dealt with by specialists in dyslexia. But, class teachers do need to be able to recognise these problems when faced with them, and have certain practical ideas in order to teach appropriately and advise on appropriate specialists for assessment.

Suggestions are given for when it may be advisable to make contact with other professional people. It is important that there are close links among professionals, and especially important that parents' views, too, are taken into account. If these links are forged with speech and language therapists, dyslexia specialists, orthoptists and others, the demands on a busy class teacher could be greatly alleviated. They would receive advice and back-up for various children who do not fit into the average learning pattern.

Everyone has two eyes, a nose and a mouth, yet – incredibly – every face is different. It follows that we are all constitutionally different and there should be no cause for surprise that we tend to acquire knowledge in different ways; there are always some things that each of us has difficulty in mastering.

Every one of us has learning difficulties in some form or another. No one is neurologically perfect, and consequently everyone has strengths and weaknesses in his or her make-up. This seems obvious but does tend to be overlooked. The fluent reader and good speller may be at a disadvantage when confronted with a musical score or a sewing-machine or a car engine. To then be called 'learning disabled' or to be said to have a learning disability would be considered grossly inappropriate and unfair. Yet, this is what may happen to the child with reading and spelling problems.

If you are disconcerted when faced with the workings – or mis-workings! – of a machine or a computer and someone comes along and explains them simply and clearly in terms that can be understood, you become more confident. With practice you start to get the idea and, in time, may become quite proficient. You can, of course, probably get by in life without being able to repair a sewing machine or read a musical score, whereas it is a very serious disadvantage if you cannot read and something of a stigma and inconvenience if you are a bad speller. There are other difficulties associated with dyslexia which are written about in this book.

Difficulties with reading and spelling, and associated problems, are known as 'specific learning disability' or 'dyslexia' – or as 'learning disabled' in the United States, and occasionally in the United Kingdom too. Fortunately, 'learning disabled' is often referred to as 'LD', and this is beginning to be accepted as 'learning different', which seems a far more positive term.

Terms such as 'specific learning disability' or 'dyslexia' – or 'learning disabled' – may be mentioned by educational psychologists, teachers, parents and others, while the child is standing there becoming quietly worried about what could be wrong with him. He knows that he is not keeping up with his peers and anxiety can begin to erode his self-confidence, and self-confidence is very important to a child's development.

It needs to be explained to him (either child or adult) that

- we all have things that we are good at and things that we have difficulty with;
- he is no different from anyone else in this way, but
- it is important to be able to read and to spell because it is a necessary part of life – and consequently of the school curriculum – therefore
- he needs help and this is not because he is stupid or lazy –

and

- there is nothing wrong with him that cannot be put right;
- furthermore, with the right sort of help – in the way that he can learn – he can begin to get on top of the problem,
- but he will have to work hard.

This explanation gives a child hope and he begins to see a light at the end of the dark tunnel. *With help and hope children are usually very willing to work hard.*

The benefits of a label

If after an assessment a child is told that he is dyslexic and is given a positive explanation of what this means, he knows then that he is *not* stupid and that he is *not* lazy, and that something can be done to help him. So often, later in children's lives this moment has been traced back to being a turning point, when lack of confidence and despair have been replaced by a growing determination to succeed. In some schools there is still antipathy towards the concept of dyslexia. The attitude is often that dyslexia is used by middle-class parents as a cover-up for a child who is not very bright or who is lazy. It does, though, seem fundamental to good teaching to recognise that all of us do not learn things in the same way. In areas other than literacy this seems to be accepted without query. Nobody argues that the inability to sing in tune is due to stupidity or laziness. Literacy problems, however, produce entirely different reactions.

Throughout the centuries the ability to read and write has been – quite wrongly – linked with intelligence. It was priests who were literate; they read the scriptures and copied and translated theological texts. Children of the aristocracy and at the manor house had governesses who usually ensured that they acquired a proficiency in literacy and numeracy. These people tended to be put on a pedestal and respected for their positions in society and for their evident intelligence and ability. In this way competence in reading and writing became linked with intelligence and social position. Conversely, the inability to read and write was linked with lack of education and apparent stupidity. It is just this attitude that has been handed down to us over the centuries and which, even today, is difficult to eradicate. It is the ability to comprehend and use knowledge which indicates intelligence. In more recent years there has been an emphasis on norms in education. It is often forgotten that these statistical norms include the backward and most advanced pupils. Norms are useful as an indication of the average ability and are used as a guide in the National Curriculum in the UK. Tests are useful provided that the results are interpreted with a view to giving a child the tuition that will enable him to improve his standards. If he does badly, *he must not just be considered a failure. Something must be done!*

But, a word of warning – and a very important one! An obvious psychological problem may cloud the picture and over-emphasise one aspect of an assessment. Children – like adults – are complex in their make-up. A learning difficulty may be put down to an experience such as adoption, parents' divorce, changing schools several times and, therefore, other causes like dyslexia or dyspraxia may lie undetected. Consequently, the child does not receive the necessary support and understanding. It is for this reason that there needs to be co-operation among professional people, and it is essential that class teachers are aware of the possibility of a variety of causes for a child's learning difficulties. It is also essential for it to be recognised that, for instance, a child might be assessed as having a speech and language processing problem, but with specific tuition he may overcome many difficulties, but still need treatment for dyslexia. For instance, his ability to express himself and comprehend could be greatly improved, but his reading and spelling will still need attention.

Dyslexia and ways of learning

Much has been said and written about good reading schemes and less good reading schemes, the various methods of teaching reading and spelling, and the best equipment with which to put across basic numeracy. Little has been said about the different ways in which people function. To give an example, a Look-Say reading scheme will no doubt be excellent for children who mentally take photographs of words as they read; these are the children who have good visual recall for words. It is as though they have a very good mental camera with an excellent lens which records the letters of a word clearly in their memories. When they see the word again on a different line or page they recognise it immediately from the mental picture called forth in their mind's eye. When they need to write it they know exactly what letters – and their correct order – to put down, and the hand usually glides effortlessly across the page. There is nothing very clever about this; it just happens that a person is constitutionally made with the skills that are needed for literacy. If you have a different make-up, then that same Look-Say reading scheme may *for you* be a disaster, as each word may need to be decoded instead of being recognised. Similarly, a phonological difficulty (that is, a difficulty building up an awareness of speech sounds and linking them to the written word) makes a purely phonic approach inappropriate.

Spelling for those with no – or poor – visual recall for words is very often an enormous problem as, particularly without a knowledge of phonics and language structure, children usually have no notion of what to put on paper. It is like finding yourself in a strange country without a map and being expected to find your way about.

There are, however, some people with no visual recall for words who somehow manage to spell correctly, often through chunking the syllables, but often also they are unable to analyse how they do it.

These difficulties also affect handwriting. Sometimes the image of the letter can be neither recalled nor linked to the relevant sound, so the writer is at a loss as to what is required. On the other hand, he may visualise the letter but be uncertain how to form it, and also be unsure of the order of the letters of a word.

Numeracy is affected too. The formation of numbers and their direction is often a problem, as well as learning multiplication tables and the order of arithmetical operations.

This ability to sequence verbal and symbolic material correctly (that is, to get information in the correct order) is definitely enhanced by the ability to visualise in the mind's eye. It is also important to know the order of the days, months and seasons. Orientation, in the sense of getting things the right way round, is important when map-reading, finding one's way, knowing right from left. Many people may have the odd quirk – perhaps confuse right and left or be unsure of letters, for instance at the end of the alphabet – but a dyslexic person tends to have a sufficient number of such difficulties to make life very uncomfortable, resulting also in loss of self-confidence.

With a little bit of discussion and questioning, a class teacher can soon begin to find out something of how children function. Discuss with them what they can see around them, including books and words in books. Then point out that they may be able to shut their eyes and *see* these objects, including words, in their minds. Ask them to close their eyes and try to do this. The teacher asks, **If I say 'cat' what can you see?** (Do not say, **If I say the** word **'cat'**, as this may be misleading.) Some may see a picture of a cat, and some will give graphic details. Then – in a neutral tone – ask, **Do you see any letters to go with your picture? What letters do you see? Does anyone see the word?** – and no picture? It is possible that they may not have understood completely the teacher's request the first time, and so the question should be put again with, perhaps, dog, fish, elephant or whatever may be appropriate for the age of the class or group. If the child sees a picture of a cat, is he also able to bring the letters to mind? Perhaps he can be seen quietly mouthing the letter-sounds and converting them into written letters. He is therefore relying on phonics. Some children are able to visualise the letter-content of words such as 'dog', 'cat' and even 'fish', but as soon as they become longer or more complex they revert to pictures. Some *see* nothing, and just occasionally one might *see* colours – for example, for an elephant the reply might be **I see a greyish colour.** Some, too, can visualise both words and objects/ scenes.

Initially, a teacher must emphasise that there are no right and wrong answers and that she is only interested in the way each child does these things. It is, of course, easier if this exercise can be carried out in small groups.

Many teachers who have a good mental image of words may not realise that others simply cannot do this. They may begin to realise, though, that they themselves have not necessarily a good visual recall for other symbols. Has the reader, for instance, an accurate mental image of the road signs for double bends, or a roundabout, or the National Westminster Bank logo? Can the reader clearly recall pictures of objects, or colours?

Children who visualise only in pictures are often the artists of the future, and the architects, designers, engineers who have practical and artistic skills. Many of them may not be able to spell correctly but they have much to offer in their lives – and any community certainly needs them! Dyslexic people are also to be found in other professions such as accountancy and medicine – though often with a good and dependable secretary! In this way it can be seen that dyslexic people have *different learning abilities* rather than a learning disability.

The dyslexic child's feelings

It is worth repeating that difficulties with reading, spelling and hand-writing may have nothing to do with intelligence (see Chapter 2, IQs). Such difficulties can be found in a person of any IQ, from low through to high. They are, though, easier to spot in a brighter person because his literacy difficulties surprise parents and teachers. Professor Tim Miles, who has done much research into dyslexia, often says of the dyslexic child's performance, **It just doesn't seem to add up!** The brighter the child, the more frustrated he can become. He cannot analyse why he cannot cope. His friends seem to be able to read and spell without any problem. Why can't *he*? If teachers tell him either that he's stupid or lazy, or even merely fail to provide reassurance to the contrary, he comes to believe just that.

Conclusions

Thirty individuals in a class cannot each have a tailor-made curriculum to follow, and teaching practices have evolved to suit the majority. However, there needs to be recognition of certain types of difficulty, strengths and weaknesses.

It is said that in every classroom there is a dyslexic child; it is prob-able, of course, that in many classes there are more than one. The situation is often masked when a very bright child gets by as average and is told that he must improve his spelling, handwriting and reading accuracy. Class teachers and subject teachers cannot be expected to give enough indi-vidual attention to any one pupil experiencing difficulties, but recognition of the learning difficulty and support in the form of learning strategies can do much for the confidence of a dyslexic child in class. Fortunately, it is being recognised that certain physical exercises can greatly improve a child's ability to learn. These are now taking place in more and more schools with very beneficial results.

As language, literacy and numeracy are important in the school curriculum and progress in other subjects is dependent on a good foun-dation in these areas, this book has been written in order to provide – in simple, jargon-free terms – information for the class teacher from day to day.

Chapter 2

Ears, eyes and IQs

In order to be sure that a learning difficulty is not being aggravated, it is always worth checking that neither eyes nor ears are causing further problems. In any case here might lie the cause of a non-dyslexic child's difficulties with reading.

Ears

Small children get stuffed up with catarrh in their noses and ears. This, in turn, can reduce the clarity of their hearing. Some children have fluctuating hearing loss if they happen to have a cold.

Glue ear

Glue ear (a chronic catarrhal condition in which the air passages are blocked) may result in the doctor recommending the insertion of grommets to clear the condition. If a child has had grommets inserted, he may well have missed out on early language development, and some of the speech and language recommendations may be appropriate, even though he is not dyslexic. Many children suffer from glue ear in their infancy and this intermittent loss can cause delay in acquiring speech and language skills. The sounds received can be distorted or even not heard; this means that the brain does not get practice at discriminating or processing sound.

If there is any question of a child not hearing properly – either because of glue ear or for any other reason – a doctor may advise a proper check at an Audiology Unit attached to a hospital. Through this it can be ascertained at what point on the decibel scale, if any, a hearing loss occurs.

High and low frequency losses

The decibel scale goes from very low frequency through to high frequency sounds, and the child's reactions, or lack of reaction if he does not hear, are noted. Speech sounds also vary from very low frequency (vowel sounds) and low frequency (**g**) to high frequency (**f, r, th** and especially **s**). If, for instance, a child has a high frequency hearing loss, he will not hear these unvoiced (whispered) letter-sounds in words spoken. This unawareness of certain sounds will affect his speech, comprehension and language development generally, besides his reading and of course spelling, if he is relying on the sounds in a word.

If a child fails to hear properly, he may not be able to concentrate on the teacher and can acquire bad listening habits which aggravate the situation. Conversely, if he does not concentrate, he will not hear and may *appear* to have a hearing loss.

Ear dominance can be a major factor in children lacking attention and understanding in the classroom. Why? Because the best scenario for a human being is to be right ear dominant. Sounds heard with the right ear travel to the major language centre situated in the left hemisphere of the brain where they are interpreted and acted upon. Left ear dominance, however, means that sounds travel to a sub-language centre on the right side of the brain and have to be transferred to the left side to be interpreted. This process takes slightly longer and the subsequent time lag – even if only for a millisecond – can affect the hearing of instructions, spelling, sequencing and understanding.

Sound therapy, which consists of a daily 10-minute session listening to specially prepared tapes of electronic music, can help with speech difficulties and sequencing problems as well as reading and spelling.

Eyes

Research has highlighted the fact that a child may have certain eye defects which could adversely affect his progress in reading.

There are three main vision skills needed for a child to read and write efficiently. The following shows some of the points to be considered:

- CONVERGENCE

  When reading and writing (and this includes spelling), the two eyes converge on letters at a distance of about 30 centimetres/12 inches. This ensures the brain receives a unified picture of the word.

- ACCOMMODATION

  The image of a word must be sharply focused. The child must be able rapidly and effortlessly to adjust the focus to the changing eye-to-print distances as he progresses along and down the page and, presumably, to the changing size of print.

Some signs of convergence/accommodation difficulty:

1 Tiredness and possible headaches as the day wears on.
2 Slowness and difficulty in copying from the board or overhead projector, or even a textbook alongside the writer. (However, a dyslexic child has a problem visualising a whole word and therefore will have this difficulty in any case.)
3 Tendency to screw up the eyes or rub the eyes, or watery eyes.
4 Bizarre spelling, with reversals, **may** indicate not only poor visual recall, but also an eye imbalance and difficulties with accommodation.

- **TRACKING, i.e. scanning along a line of print**
  When reading, not only do we scan from word to word, but also our eyes must make the larger movements from one line to another without our losing place.

Some signs of tracking/scanning difficulty:

1 A tendency to lose place or line while reading, resulting in a need to use a finger or marker to keep the place.
2 Tendency to miss out letters or words.
3 Tendency to mis-order letters within words: e.g. from/form, begin/being; and numbers, e.g. 35 for 53.

It is important for the child to have a good directional awareness and appreciate that he is always working from left to right as he reads and writes.

Tracking exercises, in which a child scans lines of print, either putting a line through the letters of the alphabet in their correct order, or through groups of letters such as **ing**, or all the **that**s, and so on, are excellent for training left-to-right eye movements, as well as scrupulous observation of letters. The child must always progress along each line, as this progression is an important part of the exercise.

For example,

> Once upon ⱥ time a furry ƀlaȼk cat went ɖown a holȼ under the ʄence at the bottom of the ǥarden. . . .

Visual defects affect reading, writing and spelling. It is often thought by eye specialists that spelling is inaccurate because the child does not see the word clearly. It then follows that an accurate image of the word has not been impressed on the mind and the view of some specialists is that this is the *cause* of dyslexia. How is it, though, that people with good recall for words (namely, accurate readers and spellers) are often unable to recall clearly the roundabout sign, National Westminster Bank logo and other similar symbols mentioned in Chapter 1, Dyslexia? It cannot be stressed too strongly that nature has not made us all in the same way and that there are plenty of people who naturally visualise in pictures and scenes, and even in some cases in colours. Because of this ability they may be more at home drawing and painting and being creative artistically than writing and reading.

The angle of a child's head when looking at a page of print or when writing can also be an indication of an eye problem. Lying sprawled across the desk *may* be a bid to cut out the use of one eye because of, for instance, a problem of eye convergence, rather than laziness. In fact, the angle of the head in relation to the book is important for both reading *and* writing; indeed, the position of the child in relation to the board is equally important.

Mixed dominance and cross-laterality

Some children may have a mixed dominance of right and left for hand, foot, eye and ear. Cross-laterality is, for instance, the way a baby should eventually crawl – left hand, right knee, right hand, left knee (see page 47).

Irlen lenses/colorimeter

Helen Irlen in the United States found that some poor readers at high school and university had what has become known as 'scotopic sensitivity'. Their eyes are sensitive to black print on white paper, especially the shine of faint black print on glossy white paper under fluorescent lighting. For them the words appear to move around on the page and may even appear to slip over the edge. The glare from the page can cause eye irritation resulting in tiredness with, perhaps, the urge to rub the eyes, streaming eyes or headaches.

In the same way as the glare of the sun can be modified if people wear sunglasses, so with certain tinted lenses the glare can be eradicated from a page of print. In order to find a person's preferred colour he is taken through a series of colour shades used as overlays on print, each time given a choice and asked for his preference. It is interesting to see how a child may suddenly find the right colour for him and say something to the effect of: **Oh! the words are still now!**

A crude test can be done with a few coloured plastic sheets over a child's reading book, and often there is a definite colour preference. Some children find it helpful to keep such a sheet to hand, as with its use they tire less quickly, can concentrate better and work far longer, particularly when faced with exam revision.

Nevertheless, however dramatic the improvement with the eyes may be, appropriate tuition is essential as well.

Eye specialists

If, when a child is trying to read, any eye discomfort is suspected, it is worth his parents asking for an appointment with an eye specialist who is particularly interested in this work. A referral from the child's doctor may be required. A teacher may be alerted to indications of discomfort if he rubs his eyes, appears to try and anchor his place with his index finger, or holds his head at an odd angle to the page.

Testing by an eye specialist should be part of every school's health check. The following are the different types of eye specialists:

Orthoptist	Measures muscle defects; usually works under an ophthalmologist and has to be approved by him or her; some work independently and recommend eye exercises where appropriate.
Ophthalmic optician/ optometrist	Looks at a wider range than an orthoptist and can prescribe spectacles and/or eye exercises; trained to recognise disease and abnormality.
Ophthalmologist	Medical consultant, mostly working in hospitals; eye surgeon dealing with eye diseases.
Optician	Supplies spectacles, but does not have to be qualified.

The eye problems described in this chapter may for some non-dyslexic children be the *cause* – or for dyslexic children be an *additional* cause – of reading difficulty and spelling problems.

IQs

It is the prerogative of parents to get their child's learning difficulties assessed by a chartered educational psychologist. This, of course, may well be at the suggestion of a teacher at the child's school. In the maintained sector this is usually arranged through the headteacher who contacts the School Psychological Service. This service may also be contacted directly by parents. In the independent sector the head of the school will be able to suggest the names of one or two chartered educational psychologists practising in the area. The educational psychologist will then be able to determine through certain tests where the child's learning strengths and weaknesses lie.

British Ability Scales and Wechsler Intelligence Scale for Children

Two forms of assessment commonly used by psychologists are the British Ability Scales (BAS) and the Wechsler Intelligence Scale for Children (WISC-R or WISC III). The main reason for administering these tests is to find out a child's *potential* academic ability. This is useful information if a child is failing to come up to expectations in class. However, the result in the form of a straight IQ figure is of limited use in itself and the sub-test scores should be considered carefully.

The British Ability Scales is comprised of a number of sub-tests which assess various cognitive functions, such as Speed of Information Processing. The Wechsler Intelligence Scale for Children is divided into two sections: the Verbal IQ and the Performance IQ. Each of these IQs is based on either five or six sub-test scores, with optional extra sub-tests. The Full Scale IQ is based on how the child functions on the test as a whole, including both Verbal and Performance sub-tests.

The majority of children are of average ability and will have more or less average results on all the sub-test scores; a very bright, academically able child will have high scores on these sub-tests and a child with low ability will have scores that are below average.

For dyslexic children and those with some other learning difficulties, these sub-test scores are not evenly distributed and, in fact, may vary considerably, resulting in what is often known as a 'spiky profile'.

From this pattern of mixed scores an educational psychologist – and an experienced teacher – will be able to see where a child's strengths and weaknesses in the learning pattern lie. For many dyslexic children, scores on Information, Arithmetic, Digit Span and Coding are low in comparison with the other sub-test scores of the WISC; hence, (A)rithmetic, (C)oding, (I)nformation, (D)igit Span. This is often known as the **ACID** profile. It is typical – though not always standard – for a dyslexic child.

Not all children are seen by chartered educational psychologists and may be tested by suitably qualified teachers within school. Here again, the importance of the details of the test – the **hows and whys** of the scores – provide the useful information, rather than the final score.

Raven's Progressive Matrices

As mentioned in Chapter 3, Speech and Language Processing, Raven's Progressive Matrices is referred to as a test of observation and clear logical thinking. There are two separate pattern-solving tests:

1   Raven's Coloured Progressive Matrices (1984) which is shorter (36 items) and geared to children up to and including 11 years;

2   Raven's Standard Progressive Matrices (60 items) which may be administered to children of 6 years onwards, including adults.

The latter is lengthy for small children, and for them the shorter Coloured Test is preferable.

As a non-verbal test, with minimal instructions, it provides useful information on a person's ability to think clearly and logically, sometimes referred to as **g-factor**.

It should be stressed that Raven's Matrices does not necessarily confirm the intelligence results of the Wechsler Intelligence Scale for Children or British Ability Scales, as it tests a different kind of intelligence – more of a common-sense than an academic type of intelligence. Another advantage of this test is that it is not timed, and therefore the child who needs time to think things through will not be penalised. If a child – or adult – with learning difficulties gains an average or low average IQ on the Wechsler Intelligence Scale for Children or British Ability Scales tests, it is worth checking to see if this is confirmed by giving that person Raven's Coloured or Standard Progressive Matrices Test. There are often surprising results. Non-Verbal Reasoning Tests are similar in that they are pattern-solving tests requiring observation and logical thinking. Another pattern-solving test now available is MAT (Matrix Analogies Test).

In general, there has been too much trust in the complete reliability of intelligence tests without giving consideration to the fact that tests are geared to various aspects of intelligence and ability. They can only ever be an attempt to assess that indefinable and elusive substance called 'intelligence', 'mental acuity' or 'shrewdness'. The result must be seen as a part of **the whole picture of the individual**.

Verbal Reasoning Tests

Verbal Reasoning Tests are widely used in schools for the purpose of allocating children to different sets. They are *not* IQ tests, but are useful indicators of a facility in processing written language. Those who achieve high scores do have the ability to do well in terms of the school's academic curriculum. However, a low score, while indicating the likelihood of certain difficulties with the curriculum, does *not* necessarily mean that the child lacks intelligence. Most children, on arrival at their secondary schools, will be given Cognitive Assessment Tests (CATS) which include verbal reasoning. Some children are handicapped by the time factor; others may find particular difficulty with the sections requiring good sequencing skills. A careful look at the test papers can provide useful pointers to specific areas of learning difficulty in an individual. Children with a weakness in language processing are bound to find verbal reasoning particularly difficult.

Memory

The phrase '*poor short-term memory*' is one that often occurs in reports and discussions on children with dyslexic difficulties. But, one needs to ask 'poor short-term memory for what?'. A child who has difficulties remembering how to spell a word or do a sum may remember very well that he has been promised an ice cream after the lesson. It could be said that most of us have a selective memory.

Dyslexic people sometimes have poor auditory memories, but many people remember numbers, such as account numbers, from many years ago. However, the digits of the Digit Span Test on the WISC, where a person is given an increasing number of haphazard digits to remember, may well be transferred from the auditory to the visual memory and then may become a test of visual recall.

The way individuals function is extremely important and will form the basis of how they memorise information and learn.

The inability to form a mental image of (visualise) words can be interpreted as having a *poor visual memory*; or, to hold a sequence of spoken digits or words as a *poor auditory memory*. It stands to reason that a child who is having to concentrate hard on the mechanics of his work may lose part of the content, and then be considered to have a bad memory for the work he has been doing in class. This is why the emphasis on teaching the dyslexic child is multi-sensory – using as many learning channels as possible to establish a working memory.

The ability to visualise in pictures can be put to good use too, and be used as hooks or connections. Tony Buzan's book *Use Your Head* gives detailed suggestions on this technique.

Conclusions

It might seem obvious that points mentioned in this chapter should be given attention. However, so often limited resources and daily pressures on people's time mean that many children go unchecked. This can add unnecessarily to both their problems and those of their teachers.

Chapter 3

Speech and language processing

One of the criticisms of the term 'dyslexia' is the difference in interpretation by various professional bodies. Teachers need to be aware of the wide range of *specific* learning difficulties and the *specific* needs each child has. As mentioned in the Introduction, the term 'dyslexia' has been used in this book because it seems to be the most apt term and is widely employed. It refers to difficulties with words read, words spelt, words pronounced, words written and the association of meanings with words, but a speech and language processing problem also needs to be taken into account. (Occasionally the term 'dysphasia' is used in reports on these children, though this is not the same as the clinical use of the word when, for instance, it is applied to stroke patients.) It is here, in particular, that the work of speech and language therapists overlaps with that of dyslexia specialists. This overlap between professions often happens in education.

It is generally recognised that many dyslexic children have a weakness in language processing. They tend to misuse words and often find it difficult to comprehend text. In some chartered educational psychologists' reports a mild speech and language processing problem is often considered to be part of the dyslexia pattern and not highlighted as a specific area of weakness. A low score on Speaking and Listening Attainment Targets, as found in the National Curriculum, may alert a teacher. A speech and language therapist then may confirm this area of weakness by the child's score on the BPVS (British Picture Vocabulary Scale).

These are the children – and adults – who have, to a greater or lesser degree, poor *short-term auditory memory* and poor *auditory discrimination* and their *auditory recall* (phonological) skills are weak. They may confuse words of similar sound, mispronounce polysyllabic words, get the stress on the wrong syllable (beat) and have no feeling for the rhythm of language. Neither can they recall a set of instructions – especially in the correct order – nor recall a story, or a sequence of events, and have difficulty remembering what they have heard from their teacher in a lesson. It is better to consider poor auditory recall as an aspect of a language disorder which needs particular attention before reading and spelling problems are tackled. Otherwise one is trying to build on an unsure foundation.

These children may even have acquired a basic Look-Say vocabulary. Nevertheless, they are limited to the words they have seen and been taught and cannot make the jump to decoding or encoding unfamiliar but phonically regular words. These are words built up from the sounds of the letters, for example, **hat, moth, soft** – not **laugh, knee, special.**

From the teaching point of view language processing problems need to be understood. Acquisition of speech sounds usually takes place early in a child's development. The table on page 18 gives an idea of the evolvement of language in the average child.

It must always be remembered that the average includes those in advance and those who are rather behind in their development, and there should not be undue alarm if a child is a little late in language achievement.

Many people consider, though incorrectly, that the work of speech and language therapists deals only with the correction of sounds wrongly articulated and pronounced; for example, **My sister Wose has wed hair; My bruvver finks he knows it all.** Correcting such wrong articulation is, of course, an important aspect of a child's speech. Eccentric pronunciation may sound rather sweet in a 3–4 year old, but can be very irritating if left uncorrected and is still present at 8–9 years.

When a small child talks about **bummy rabbits** or **canker m'diggers** (mechanical diggers) it is thought to be amusing. Sometimes such mistakes get taken up endearingly into family vocabulary. When an 8-year-old boy playing cops and robbers shouts, '**Bang, Bang, Bang, You're deadicated!**', or a 12-year-old girl opening a shortened version of Jane Eyre says, '**Oh, this is a different virgin!**' or an adult remarks, '**Some swimming pools are warm and others are isolated**' or '**He'd give his high teeth to get a good job**', it is funny, but such mistakes need to be explained and rectified.

Most young children naturally grow out of this type of mistake. Parents and teachers explain and they rectify them without much difficulty. But if these problems of mispronunciation or use of the wrong word are prolific and continue, then advice and help are needed. A speech and language therapist will advise on how best to get the child to *listen* and then *produce* correct pronunciation. Children with spelling difficulties rely on word-sounds when writing, so correct pronunciation is very important. Teachers, and also parents, must learn to *listen* to a child's speech. It is all too easy to accept it uncritically and be unaware of mistakes in the use of language, thinking only of what the child is communicating.

There is another aspect of language development – and therefore of a speech and language therapist's work – which deals with speech and

General guide to average language development

Age

Up to I year   Babbling.

1–2 years   Is able to:
  respond to name and 'no';
  recognise names of common objects;
  identify common pictures when named;
  use combinations of two or more words;
  follow simple instructions.

2–3 years   Is able to:
  name common pictures;
  identify action in pictures;
  repeat two random digits;
  understand well in advance of speech and enjoy simple
    familiar stories.

3–4 years   Is able to:
  repeat three random digits;
  say at least one nursery rhyme;
  understand basic grammatical structure even if using
    goed, wented and mans, etc.

4–5 years   Is able to:
  repeat four random digits;
  carry out three instructions given together;
  repeat 12-syllable sentences;
  speak intelligibly.

5–6 years   Receptive vocabulary is such that he enjoys longer and
    complex stories;
  basic grammar is complete;
  is developing powers of reasoning and criticism.

6–7 years   Is able to:
  tell a familiar story or give an account of an event.
  Late speech errors should diminish, e.g. lisped s and f/th
    confusions.

7–8 years   Is able to:
  repeat five random digits;
  absorb and process information.

language processing. Speech and language therapy is highly specialised work, and the following is a non-technical and simplified analogy of some of the problems dealt with. It is by such an analogy that the reader may be helped to understand these problems.

Analogy of speech and language processing problems

Most children learn to use their mother tongue with facility – they learn to use words correctly, construct sentences, understand replies, follow a family discussion. For some this does not come easily at all. We merely have to imagine ourselves in a foreign country, say France, with a reasonable but limited amount of French. We need to buy bread, for instance, and before going into the shop we work out the vocabulary to construct a sentence or two. Faced with Madame behind the counter we carefully, and rather anxiously, communicate what we want. But, was the pronunciation of **pain** correct, or did it sound more like the English **pain**? Has she understood? Is she laughing as she turns her back to reach for the bread? Next, the bread is on the counter and we feel we're making progress – but what is she saying as she hands it over? Is she commenting on the weather or saying something about the price? We sort that out, and before leaving the shop, ask the way to the **gare** with much gesticulation. She understands, and there then proceeds a volley of French which we understand to be helpful directions. We recognise a word here and there but cannot remember the meaning. Outside the shop we stand and cogitate. Was it the third road on the right, or was it right at the roundabout? Finally, after half an hour, instead of the fifteen minutes we're sure she said, we arrive at the station where there is considerable bustle. We decide to get something to read, but everyone is talking at once at the bookstall and it is just impossible to sift the information we want out of the cross-fire of chat. Finally, we decide it's not worth the hassle of trying to buy a newspaper or magazine and, feeling thwarted and inadequate, we just give up.

Many people have experienced such a situation when travelling abroad, and it is just these kinds of difficulties that children with speech and language processing problems are experiencing daily in their first language.

Learning difficulties

An *expressive language difficulty* results in problems putting thoughts into words; a *receptive language difficulty* results in being unable to follow adequately the language of others. Some children may have both an expressive and a receptive language difficulty.

These children may have been slow to pick up speech, and some of them will already have had speech and language therapy at the pre-school stage. They will probably continue to have the following problems:

1 Mispronunciation of words; e.g. the **bummy** rabbit type of mistake will persist. (*Expressive*)

2 Confusion over similar-sounding words such as **lemon/melon**. (*Expressive*)

3 Misunderstanding the meanings of words well within the capability of their age range; for example, a 9-year-old girl had written in her workbook, alongside a picture of a ship going down below the waves, **The ship sinks**. As the lesson was to do primarily with reading, writing and spelling, there was no apparent problem. However, when discussing this picture later the child was asked for the meaning of the word **sink**, and she replied that it was where you washed up the dishes! Consequently, **the ship sinks** had no meaning for her. (Receptive)

   Likewise, in a reading book there was a story about a bandit planning to rob a bank. On the way there he was pushed by the hero over into a ravine where he lay **limp and still**. Asking a child what **limp** meant, it was not uncommon to get the reply: '**It's when you hurt your leg and you then limp.**' The dramatic ending of the story was lost.

4 A young child learning colours, for instance, may have no problem in picking out the blue bricks, or matching them to others, but may find it extremely difficult to give the correct response when asked, 'What colour is this?'. (*Expressive*)

5 Confusion over and mispronunciation of people's names – **Mr Robson/Robinson/Robertson; or Mr What's-his-name.** (*Expressive*)

6 Problems comprehending the meanings of prepositions or connectives, such as **in/on/under, in front/behind** (see Chapter 10, Orientation). (*Receptive*)

7 **Confusion of** verb tenses and time:
   a **I have done it soon**
   b **I will do it yesterday**

and understanding the passive tense:

   a **Ann was teased by Jack**
   b **Bill was hit by Stephen**

which reverses the usual order of subject–verb–object. According to Professor David Crystal the passive tense is not normally comprehended by the average child before 7½ years. For the child with speech and language processing problems it may be considerably later. The passive tense, though, can be found in some early Readers. (*Receptive*)

8　Difficulty in using verb tenses and sentence structure. A 9-year-old boy arrived for his lesson, and announced, '**Skipping worns out me!**'. (*Expressive*)

9　Difficulty learning nursery rhymes, and later poetry, multiplication tables, and so on. (*Expressive*)

10　Confusion in processing two or three requests or instructions; e.g. '**Take off your boots, go and wash your hands and come to the kitchen for tea.**' Or, '**Sit down, take out your English book, turn to page 25 and do Exercise 3.**' (*Receptive*)
　　It is as though the brain gets overloaded with words and the child cannot process it all. In the first example he may latch on to the last bit about tea and then be found sitting at the table with dirty hands and his muddy boots still on. In the second example he might well be sitting looking at page 3 in his English book and wondering what to do.

11　Failure to understand:

　　　　proverbs – such as, **when one door shuts, another door opens**

　　　　euphemisms – such as, **popping his clogs**

　　　　idioms – such as, **throwing the baby out with the bath water** or **opening his mouth and putting his foot in it.** (*Receptive*)

These sayings tend to be taken literally. For instance, a busy mother asked her son to **give her a hand,** and was surprised to see him standing with his hand held out.

12　Failure, too, to pick up nuances or '**vibes**', which leads him into trouble with accusations of being cheeky when he has not appreciated that comment is inappropriate (see Chapter 4, ADD and Dyspraxia). (*Receptive and expressive*)

13　Persistent difficulties in pronouncing polysyllabic words such as **hostipal** (hospital), **syllophosical** (philosophical), and forever coming up with spoonerisms such as **parcark, flutterby, sgapetti, crinimal.** Also, confusing two similar words such as **accept** and **except;** or **affect** and **effect**; or, **askance** and **ensconce** and coming up with a different word like **enskance**, and then being unsure of its meaning! (*Expressive*)

14 Difficulty finding the correct word and always using such terms as **thingummy-jig** and **what's-its-name**. (*Expressive*)

It is often not understood that these children, and adults too, need more time to produce information or to comprehend. They require a slower pace of conversation, based on familiar vocabulary, as their own core vocabulary is limited. Because of difficulty in retrieving words (that is, recalling the word wanted), use of spoken vocabulary is immature and restricted – and even more so in written work where the child may limit himself even further to what he can spell. Difficulties in taking in information in class may well be compared with the sort of problems described earlier in the analogy of a trip to France.

Such difficulties with both expressive and receptive language can undermine all attempts at academic work and social relationships. These children are prevented from thriving because they cannot communicate adequately. If everyone else is involved in a discussion and such a child cannot take part, then he may well opt out, perhaps gaze out of the window and become known as a dreamer. During family discussions at home he may withdraw to his bedroom. At school he may play alone in the playground. Remarks like '**He's a bit of a loner**' often follow. Parents may be informed that their child is reticent in class and should join in more. He, however, knows that he cannot retrieve the words quickly enough to compete with the others and so is unlikely to put up his hand, even when he knows the answer. Alternatively, some become fidgety and restive, disrupting the rest of the class. Occasionally, someone with such a problem may try to dominate the conversation so as not to be put in the position of trying to follow and take part.

As with all problems, an *understanding* of the problem by other people is of paramount importance. These are the children who may well irritate their teachers and parents because of their vagueness and inability to grasp meanings of words and to communicate at the expected level. This can put a great strain on their families, teachers and peers who invariably do not know how to cope with such a situation.

On one occasion a girl was accused of lying to her teacher because she gave a different version of what she had been told to do; she was recalling the instructions to the best of her ability but had misunderstood. If the language processing problem is not recognised it can well lead to a confrontation between teacher and child.

Without wishing to be dramatic, one wonders if some of those apprehended by the police always understand the statement that they sign. Moreover, if angry feelings are locked inside a person because he cannot find the words to express that anger, a physical attack may be his only resort. In such circumstances neighbours have often been heard to comment with amazement, '**But he's such a quiet man!**'.

Case study: Diana

Peter Gilchrist, a chartered educational psychologist assessed a 10½-year-old girl, Diana, and in his report he referred to her school reports which mentioned '**a vagueness and a rather butterfly mind**'. He noted the '**comparative immaturity of her language development and how easily she becomes confused in actually trying to express herself**' and continued that he was '**not at all surprised to hear that she is equally confused in class by trying to grasp what is expected of her, especially where the concept is in any way sophisticated**'. Later in his assessment report he mentioned that '**she still confuses subtly different sounds and continues to have surprising difficulty in analysing more complex words into their phonic components**'. (This would inevitably cause a difficulty in reading and spelling.) Finally, he dealt with her difficulties of comprehension and recommended that '**when a new concept is described . . . that once she appears to have understood what is required of her, she should be given a similar task and . . . "you be teacher" and explain exactly what is required**'.

If a child has a receptive language problem – that is, does not always understand what is being said and is therefore confused over instructions – he may have a low score on an intelligence test that requires verbal instructions. He may appear to be slow and dull, and it is easy to assume that this is the case when the score of the Verbal IQ appears to confirm this.

An IQ assessment on the Wechsler Intelligence Scale for Children or British Ability Scales may give a false impression of such a child's overall intelligence, and teachers and parents then lower their expectations of that child's ability. Although academic subjects will be affected, there needs to be recognition of other types of intelligence. If a speech and language processing problem is suspected, a non-verbal pattern-solving test, such as Raven's Progressive Matrices, may well reveal intelligence of a different sort. Raven's Matrices is a test of observation and clear thinking, which reflects an ability to cope with life, good common sense, possibly business acumen, sometimes perhaps a street-wise approach. Diana scored at the 85–90 percentile level, that is, the top 5–6 per cent in the country, but only achieved a Full Scale IQ of 91 – namely, low average – on the Wechsler Intelligence Scale for Children. Raven's Progressive Matrices test is available to teachers (see Chapter 2, Ears, eyes and IQs).

There is nothing new in this observation. Even Chaucer in the fourteenth century wrote in his General Prologue to the *Canterbury Tales*:

> There was a worthy Manciple [purchasing officer of provisions] of
> one of the Inns of Court who might have served as a model to carterers
> for shrewdness in the purchase of provisions; for whether he paid
> cash or bought on credit, he watched prices all the time, so that he
> always got in first and did good business.
>
> Now is it not a remarkable example of God's Grace that the wit
> of an uneducated man like this should outmatch the wisdom of a
> pack of learned men? His superiors numbered more than thirty and
> were all erudite and expert in the law ... yet this Manciple could
> hoodwink the lot of them.

Sadly, Diana did not receive much specialist tuition and when she was
13 years 9 months a speech and language therapist was called in to give
an assessment with particular reference **to her inability to remember
instructions, understand adequately what is said to her, and to communicate verbally at a level appropriate to her age and intellectual ability.** Her
parents described her as **'a girl who also has trouble relating clearly a
sequence of events, when compared to other girls of her own age. She
finds it difficult to use appropriate words in describing events so making
it difficult for the listener to follow the story.'** Moreover, her mother
recalled that Diana **'was unable to learn nursery rhymes as a child, in
spite of exposure to them and efforts to help her learn and enjoy them'**.

Had the signs of Diana's difficulties been recognised and understood
earlier in her life, she could have been helped long before she was struggling with the more demanding curriculum of a senior school and before
her confidence in social relationships had been so badly affected. There
are more children in this situation than have been generally recognised
up till now.

Fortunately, in the end Diana did receive tuition from a speech and
language therapist during her GCSE course and obtained, at age 16, seven
GCSEs – 3 Cs and 4 Ds. Two years later she achieved two A-levels – Art
at Grade C and Photography at Grade A. She chose photography as a
career and has been doing very well indeed both professionally and socially.

What class teachers can do

As all teachers know, children get teased by others and ridiculed about
their misuse and mispronunciation of words. We should think how we
feel in a foreign country, especially if foreigners start laughing at our
attempts in their language! Steps need to be taken quickly to scotch such
mockery.

The following are some suggestions for helping the child with a speech
and language processing problem, both expressive and receptive:

1 Listen carefully to the child's speech – and believe your ears! Become aware of his misused words. Correct a mispronunciation immediately and diplomatically, perhaps merely repeating the word or sentence correctly, so that the child does not feel humiliated. Embarrassment and humiliation can become more undermining than the language disorder itself. (*Expressive*)

2 Speak more slowly and face the child. Ensure that the words and expressions you use are understood. If in any doubt, repeat in a different way, and use short sentences. (*Receptive*)

3 Children need to develop good listening habits, including eye contact. Time for exchange of news in pairs or small groups is well spent. It often helps if small groups in, for instance, infant classes sit in a circle and face each other for News Time.

   Circle Time is a positive extension of the above practice and is good for children with both speech and language processing problems and behavioural problems. The activities are all intended to promote a positive self-image and help children to become aware of the needs of others in the class (see Circle Time, Chapter 4). (*Receptive and expressive*)

4 Tapping or clapping rhythms. Children may begin by tapping or clapping the syllables/beats of their own names, including emphasising any stressed syllables; for instance, **Jon-a-than, Ka-ty, Paul, Al-ex-an-der, Ja-mie**. Gradual progression should be made to words which they tend to mispronounce, and later to words that they tend to mis-spell, such as **re-mem-ber** (see Chapter 6, Spelling). (*Receptive and expressive*)

5 Nursery rhymes, poetry and times tables are more easily learnt if a child is aware of the rhythm of the language.

6 Communicating through rhythm alone. A game may be played by the teacher clapping the rhythm of a nursery rhyme or pop song and seeing who can recognise it (see Chapter 7, Spelling).

7 Ensure that the child understands the meanings of the key words when he is being spoken to and when he is reading. Ask often for the meanings of words and continue to reinforce correct meanings. Visual clues (pictures) are useful back-up to spoken or written information. Key words on cards with explanations and sketches – possibly kept at the back of his exercise book or folder – is a helpful way to provide an easy reference.

If working on a particular topic in class, the child may require the key vocabulary to be repeated several times before it is firmly established.

Older children value flow diagrams with colour support (see Chapter 7, Spelling and Chapter 12, Study Skills). (*Receptive and expressive*)

8 Many children are reluctant to admit that they have not understood the teacher as they assume that a lack of understanding is entirely their own fault. It may, in fact, be a lack of awareness by the teacher of a child's weakness in receptive language. (*Receptive*)

9 When a new concept has been introduced to the class it is helpful if, on occasions, the child with comprehension difficulties can 'be teacher' and explain the new information to someone else or on to a tape. It will then become more secure in that child's understanding. (*Receptive and expressive*)

10 A string of requests should be given separately, if possible going on to the second after the first has been accomplished, and so on. Parents' help can be enlisted to iron out confusions over such requests as '**take off your boots, then go and wash your hands**'. It is helpful to encourage children to create a picture in their minds of the information to be remembered; for instance, taking off dirty boots, seeing themselves standing at the basin and washing their hands, or, similarly, doing a task in school. '**Imagine you have a video in your head!**' (*Receptive*)

11 Try to alternate language activities with practical activities in class.

12 It often helps children to demonstrate their understanding in practical ways. They may not be able to find the correct language to classify the arranged materials – in, for instance, SATs (Standard Attainment Tests) Science – but by physically putting like with like they may show an amazing degree of understanding and achievement. These children often fail because they have misunderstood the language rather than having been unable to carry out the task. They may need to have questions repeated or re-worded. Visual stimuli should be encouraged whenever possible; for instance, use of colour with phonics, mind maps, diagrams.

13 Requests need to be constructed for such children to ensure that the meaning is really understood. Gestures by the teacher or parent often preclude the understanding of words; it is the gestures alone that are understood. Instructions such as '**You can go out to play when you have finished that page**' can be confusing because of the order in

which it is said. For some children it is better to say: **'Finish that page first and then you can go out to play'**. (*Receptive*)

14 Over a period of time the number in a string of requests can be gradually increased. This can be played as a game in class; for instance, the teacher asks a child to **'go to the front of the room, take three pencils from the desk, give one to Gavin, one to Karen and one to Stephen, then go and sit down'**. The number of requests can be varied according to the abilities of the children; and, of course, the child with a problem of language processing should be given the number that he has a good chance of achieving successfully. This can also be a useful exercise in concentration and memory for the whole class. (*Receptive*)

15 Sensitively correct wrong use of words on the spot, otherwise incorrect spoken language becomes incorrect written language, as in **'I could of done it'**. Do not allow mockery by other children, and perhaps remind them that this child may be better than they are at, for instance, art, football or IT. (*Expressive*)

16 It is often difficult to sift information from the crossfire of a discussion. In a classroom or in a family discussion, people should try to ensure that the child is involved in at least one direct remark. The child should be given time and help, and not put under pressure, for he must (a) understand, (b) find the appropriate vocabulary, and (c) string his thoughts into a grammatical construction which can be understood. All this may not come easily. Initially, a one-word response may be all that he achieves, but he has at least been included. As confidence grows he can be encouraged to attempt more complex replies. Cueing (giving the first sounds of a word that he may be trying to find) by parent or teacher may help him in the process. (*Receptive and expressive*)

17 For those who tend to become aggressive because they are unable to express their anger and resentment at certain times, a Social Language Group may be a very effective way of dealing with this situation.

In the group they are taught to become aware of acceptable ways of communicating with others. For instance, on the playground **'Hey!'** may be a recognised way of attracting the attention of a friend, but, in order to attract a teacher's attention in class **'Excuse me!'** is more appropriate. Similarly, a child should address his headteacher, his parent and his good friend differently.

This kind of awareness is important, otherwise social acceptance later in life may be put at risk. For example, when arriving at an interview for a job it is as well to know that the reply to '**Good morning, Daniel**' is '**Good morning, Mr Smith**' and not '**Hi!**'.

In the same way, in the general course of conversation it is important to be able to pick up modulations of the voice. '**Go away!**' may be said both playfully and with anger. An unawareness of this could lead to the wrong reaction. In addition, an ability to deal with criticism is essential for maintaining good social relationships.

Learning that different responses are appropriate in different circumstances is necessary. This extends to the need for different types of writing – a school essay, a letter of application, a postcard to a sibling. (See Chapter 4, ADD and dyspraxia). (*Receptive and expressive*)

18 As it is quite possible that there are a number of children in the school with speech and language processing problems which are similar, it could be both economic and advantageous to have one child assessed by a speech and language therapist who could then talk to the staff on the basis of that child's assessment. This would enable teachers to get a clearer understanding of how to treat the others as well.

Conclusions

Many people are unaware that speech and language processing is a problem for some children, and indeed for some adults too. Speech problems are often only considered if articulation is poor. The more subtle difficulties of receptive and expressive speech and language processing are so often overlooked, and a teacher then tries to improve the child's literacy, unaware that she is working on a weak foundation.

It is vital to widen vocabulary and improve the comprehension of infants before tackling their reading and spelling. Improvement in vocabulary and comprehension should be included in any tuition to raise the standard of reading and spelling in the junior and senior stages as well. Otherwise a child may be thought to be unable to communicate freely *because* of lack of confidence and social skills, rather than the lack of confidence and social skills being caused by difficulties in communication.

Clear communication – with correct understanding – is an extremely important aspect of a child's education. It is not unusual to hear two people having a heated argument along the lines of '**I didn't say that at all. I said such-and-such.**' '**No, you didn't, you said so-and-so.**' Both people are honestly sure that what they have understood is the correct meaning of the exchange. If this can happen between two adults, possibly in the same family and speaking the same language, how much greater is the chance of misunderstanding on the international scene! The ability to express thoughts clearly and unambiguously is of vital importance and should start in the classroom.

Chapter 4

ADD and dyspraxia

ADD

It is possible – though not necessarily the case – for a child to be both dyslexic and have an attention deficit disorder. The labels 'ADD' (attention deficit disorder) and 'ADHD' (attention deficit hyperactivity disorder) have become increasingly common, often giving rise – yet again – to further parental and teacher anxiety.

The child who has a problem concentrating finds life in the classroom particularly difficult – and so does the teacher!

Denise Thornton, a Chartered Educational Psychologist, who has specialised in this area of education, describes the problem as being biological and a 'developmental condition that can lead to behaviour problems because the brain does not receive all the messages it should – like a radio losing its signal.' She recommends that there is a clear set of rules for the child to follow. In this way he learns exactly what is expected of him.

There are three aspects in particular of an attention deficit disorder which may alert a parent or teacher:

1 inattention (poor concentration);
2 impulsivity;
3 hyperactivity (restlessness).

These symptoms must be of *at least six months' standing* and have been *evident since early childhood* and also *in the absence of any other significant disorder*. It has been thought that a number of these children grow out of these symptoms at puberty, but it is now believed that the symptoms change. Jenny Lyons, Specialist AD/HD Educational Psychologist writes that 'hyperactivity and impulsiveness diminish but attention problems continue. Around two thirds of children with this condition will do less well than their peers, experiencing social, vocational and relationship problems' (see PATOSS Bulletin, May 2003).

As with the label 'dyslexia', when there is an explanation for the difficulties being encountered there can be enormous relief for all concerned

– child, parents and teachers. It is then understood that there are underlying reasons for the poor concentration, impulsivity and restlessness; the
child is not merely 'naughty' and being badly managed at home. Nor is
an ADD a psychiatric disorder. However, just as every dyslexic child has
a different learning style and personality, so has every child with an ADD.
Even with a diagnostic label there are no simple answers. It is the pattern
of difficulties which must be considered. Once again, the lines between
diagnoses become blurred as the child may be experiencing other difficulties as well; for instance, frustrations encountered with speech and
language processing, literacy problems or very low self-esteem, and worrying, all of which can lead to severe concentration difficulties.

Allergies are often considered to be the reason for some behavioural
problems. However, if a test period of three weeks without the 'trigger'
in question does not produce significant improvement, allergies are unlikely
to be the cause. Nutritional balance and food allergies can both be relevant to a child's well-being and subsequent academic performance. It is
known, though, that allergies are significant in causing attentional difficulties in only a small percentage of cases. However, when they *are*
relevant, they will be of particular significance.

Similarly, a comparison can be made with dyslexia in that cases of
ADD lie along a continuum, some with severe and some with moderate
and mild difficulties.

In the playground, a child with an ADD may stand out as immature
and self-centred. He can be aggressive, may make impulsive attempts to
join groups and wish to change the rules of the game he joins. Generally,
he feels picked on by staff and peers alike – and is quite unable to see
how he has managed to bring so many of the upsets upon himself.

It may be of value to observe, if possible with the co-operation of an
assistant, which aspects of his behaviour are causing the greatest problems in class and then consider positive ways of trying to deal with these
– perhaps concentrating on one at a time. When one key area of behaviour is modified (for instance, incessant chatter), this helps to modify other
key areas and improve the child's feelings of self-confidence.

Research has shown that there is a genetic disposition to an attention
deficit disorder. It also seems reasonable that such a disorder may be exac-
erbated by stress or by a traumatic experience in early childhood. Either
of these might explain an inability to concentrate, to relate to peer group,
to accept authority and generally be considered 'impossible'. It may be
that the realistic course of action under these circumstances includes
medication. Methylphenidate (Ritalin) is the most widely administered
drug in such cases. Ritalin is a stimulant. It stimulates the brain which,
in turn, produces more of the normal chemicals which calm a child down
and so modifies behaviour. In this way it is hoped that, with the right
teaching, the child will gradually establish good relationships and, in so

doing, gain a feeling of security in relating to people. The aim is that this security will enable him eventually to be withdrawn from Ritalin. Unfortunately, many parents take advice from a paediatrician without the knowledge of the child's teachers. *It is vital that there is good communication among all those concerned with a child.*

A word of caution! There are children whose inability to concentrate may be *caused by the frustrations of their being dyslexic*. They are under pressure at school every day, and highly intelligent children *still* may be written off as stupid. A paediatrician, if he is unaware of dyslexia and its frustrations, may diagnose ADD or ADHD and prescribe a course of Ritalin which, in some cases, is administered over a period of several years. What such a child *really* needs is the right tuition and an understanding environment to enable him to be taught in the way he, as a dyslexic person, learns. A number of headteachers at schools for dyslexic children have found that, given such a situation, the apparent ADD symptoms and the need for Ritalin soon disappear. Moreover, there is still little knowledge of the effects of Ritalin in the long term. Even in the short term it has to be very carefully monitored as side effects, such as tics, loss of weight and altered sleep patterns, may result. Any advice by a paediatrician should be given in the light of information from other professional people, such as an educational psychologist and any teachers involved with the child and, of course, the parents' views and experiences. If parents first opt for medical advice, and a medical diagnosis and subsequent treatment are considered on their own, the involvement and responsibility of the child's teachers run the risk of being undermined. It is crucial that class teachers and special needs teachers who are in close daily contact with such a child are fully in the picture.

It should be remembered that whereas Ritalin and such medication can increase concentration, reduce impulsivity and lessen irrelevant physical activity, it can do nothing to remediate learning difficulties, normalise peer relationships, teach improved control or correct mismanagement. *It should never be used merely to manipulate class management as this could become a dangerous precedent.*

Thom Hartmann, who describes himself as having an attention deficit disorder, considers an interesting dimension of the cause in his book *ADD: A Different Perception*. He reminds us that original prehistoric man was a hunter, and traits necessary to be a successful hunter include an awareness of everything happening around – observing tracks, responding immediately to the sound of a twig snapping, watching a bird's flight, holding a sling ready and so on. In other words, concentration on one thing was not appropriate and could even be positively dangerous. Alertness, the courage to take risks, to make instant decisions and act upon them were characteristics of the prehistoric hunter, and all crucial to his survival.

He goes on to say that in due course some primitive men became farmers. The characteristics of farmers are quite different from hunters. They need to plan ahead, to concentrate on the task in hand, to co-operate with others in order to sow and reap, to attend to details with patience and tolerance – in short, to develop the ability to reflect and reason. Many children with a 'hunter personality' have grown into adults who are known for their innovative ideas and business enterprises, but once the new enterprise is under way it is often the 'farmer' who is needed as manager for it to survive.

Thom Hartmann considers that many of today's children and adults with an attention deficit disorder may have hunter personalities. We need to recognise these hunter temperaments. By and large they are easily distracted and restless children, always out of their seats and wandering round the classroom. They disturb others, fidget with irrelevant objects and the work they present is hasty and careless. They are disorganised, lose their possessions, make snap decisions and may take risks without weighing up the consequences. They may talk impulsively and excessively, not listen when others are speaking and frequently interrupt. They butt into situations uninvited and may find it difficult to wait for their turn in group activities. They disrupt the class and drive their teachers to despair! As one observation schedule classifies the child – a **TOAD**! He is always (**T**)alking, (**O**)ut of his seat, (**A**)ttention-seeking and (**D**)isruptive.

This hunter/farmer theory gets away from the negative terms 'deficit' and 'disorder' and leaves scope for a more positive view of the ADD and ADHD characteristics. The hunters tend to be flexible in their strategies and may think visually – that is, record incidents pictorially rather than verbally. This is a clue to teaching strategies.

Nutrition

Many children have an unhelpful diet with an excess of stimulants such as sugar or sweeteners as in diet drinks, colourings, flavourings and preservatives. We are not always aware of the contents of the things our children eat at home or at school. It is not always realised that these additives can easily upset brain function and put the child into a 'hyper' state, which can result in poor behaviour and lack of concentration. Not conducive to good performance in the classroom, when children are already struggling to read and write. Modern food processing has been partly responsible for robbing our diet of 'Essential Fatty Acids', which are essential for healthy brain functioning. However, a fish oil supplement will improve not only brain function but also visual function. Two leading researchers in this field, Dr Jacqueline Stordy and Dr Alex Richardson aim to raise awareness of the implications of diet on education and behaviour.

What class teachers and parents can do

1 A child with an ADD needs as few distractions as possible. Ideally, he should have access to a quiet area of the classroom, but be within easy range for the teacher to prompt and praise him unobtrusively.

   Earphones may be used on occasions to help cut out extraneous noise, or some older pupils are happy to carry around a cardboard 'learning bay'. This can be erected on their desks when individual work is required and helps to minimise distraction. Some pupils – often teenagers – may prefer to focus on what is being said by closing their eyes and listening.

2 Eye contact is essential before the child is given any instructions and these should be explained one at a time and in simple language.

3 A prompting code between teacher and child could be worked out so that the teacher does not seem to be nagging. Sometimes teachers can be so focused on the negative that they fail to be in any way positive. Constant disapproval and undermining of a child's confidence can lead to anti-social and violent behaviour. If possible, any reprimand should be audible only to the child and given in a matter-of-fact voice or by an agreed gesture.

4 Teachers – and parents – need to stress the positive wherever they can. Apparently children are frequently unaware of 'Don't' at the beginning of a sentence. The negative 'Don't do' is often not heard. It is better to say 'Do', e.g. 'Don't wander around the classroom' is better expressed as 'Do sit down'.

5 The teacher should be looking for moments to catch the child doing well and reward or praise any positive signs of improvement, such as when he completes a specific task or makes a positive contribution to class activities. This will help to boost his self-image and reinforce any improvement in his behaviour, ultimately leading to even greater achievement.

6 The need is for a timetable of the day's activities to be written clearly and simply so that the child knows what will happen next. In this

way the child will gain self-confidence and a feeling of security from knowing what he is expected to do. If the teacher is in any doubt about the pupil having understood, the child should be asked to repeat the instructions (see Chapter 3, Speech and language processing).

If by any chance there is a change in the timetable, this needs to be explained clearly and simply – maintaining eye contact – to lessen any confusion.

7   As with all educational matters the assessment and intervention have to be interwoven and continuous. As the ADD difficulties are as much part of the home picture as the school picture, it is vital that there is a full and on-going dialogue with all concerned with the pupil. Understanding by people such as playground assistants and lunch-time supervisors is essential for consistent, positive handling of situations. Furthermore, peer groups and friends should be included in the plans as well.

8   **Circle Time** (the activity by which a large proportion of the Personal, Social Education (PSE) curriculum is delivered in primary schools) is an excellent opportunity to include any child with an ADD in a class activity. It improves his social skills and awareness. He sits in a circle with his peers and teacher(s), where everyone is equal and can be seen and heard. He feels part of the group. It is an occasion to involve the other children who are only too aware that their classmate with an ADD is a difficult character.

The ground rules for the group are as follows:

(a)   a child may say '**pass**' if he does not want to answer;
(b)   children listen while someone else is speaking;
(c)   no one interrupts or ridicules someone else's comments.

This creates a feeling of security within the group and a respect for others. It is unacceptable to use another child's name when voicing a criticism. For example, '**I don't like Alex pushing me**' should be expressed as '**I don't like being pushed**'. In this way each child feels accepted and valued as a person. Self-esteem is enhanced and self-discipline is developed. An environment is created where, for instance, a child who chatters incessantly may be reminded by a signal from a friend to keep silent. Bit by bit he learns to curb his impulse and may begin to enjoy success.

The child with an expressive language processing problem will, in time, begin to feel confident enough to volunteer a remark rather than say '**pass**'.

Circle Time can be very flexible and be used creatively by the teacher; the concerns of the children on that day may well determine how the time is used. Sometimes new friendships are formed when one or two children realise that they view a certain comment in the same way. They learn to be honest about their views and consider others.

A teacher can sensitively encourage peer support by including the whole class and the child with an ADD in a discussion of that child's strengths. It could be suggested that his peers volunteer to help and support him over his problems. He then feels he has friends and is no longer an outcast. In this way Circle Time and peer support can both be very, very important for a child with poor social skills.

In some schools each class has Circle Time once a week. After a few weeks it has been found that social relationships are strengthened and children are monitoring themselves and reminding one another of the rules. The whole school benefits from the increased consideration for others and the general atmosphere is improved.

9 A **contract** between teacher and pupil with an ADD can have a beneficial effect. The child can then set his sights on trying hard to improve a certain aspect of his behaviour (see Social stories, pages 36–8). For instance, if a child is inclined to leave his place on impulse, he could be encouraged and reminded by those next to him, and will then try very hard to remain in his seat – perhaps starting with two to three minutes and gradually extending that time. Goals must be realistic, so to begin with the time set should be very short. He will not necessarily succeed the whole time, but with approval and possibly a reward from his teacher when he does succeed – and perhaps with enthusiastic encouragement from his peers as well – he will begin to feel good about himself. The 'feel good factor' raises self-esteem and, in turn, enhances friendships and increases self-confidence. Co-operation with both peers and adults may improve and a child increasingly becomes more sensitive to the feelings of others.

10 Parents need to work out ways of helping their child to organise his homework and put together what he needs for the following day at school.

11 Good co-operation between school and parents – for example, meeting at two- or three-weekly intervals – increases enormously the chances of success of any actions taken by a teacher to meet the needs of a child with ADD. This would also make the class teacher's work more productive and less stressful.

Social stories

'Social stories' are a means of communicating in a positive way with children who are experiencing difficulties of all kinds. They are written with a positive view of a problem that initially seems insurmountable. The pupil and an adult write the story together, in words that the pupil can not only understand, but also read for himself. If his literacy skills are very poor, the story, as written in the child's words, can be taped or read to him.

Day 1

Decide on the problem to be tackled and plan some positive things that could be done to overcome it. Create a front cover and write the first page of a loose-leaf book. This could be as short as a single sentence with an illustration.

For example, a 14-year-old boy, Ben, who was school phobic, wrote the following as the start of his story: 'When Ben reached the classroom door he took a deep breath. "I am going to look forward to my free time this evening instead of worrying about all the things I haven't done."'

Day 2

Read yesterday's instalment and add a second page. This could be to reinforce yesterday's target or add a second positive thing to do.

- Each day more can be written with new ideas for positive action, as well as re-reading the story from the beginning. The adult's task throughout the day is to keep reminding the pupil of the positive actions he is trying to achieve.
- Only one problem per storybook is allowed.
- Read it daily, as early in the day as possible.
- Pages can be rejected. If the idea has been tried and it doesn't help, pull it out!
- Pages can be inserted between existing ones if the sequence has been discussed and deemed an improvement.

Of course, this *is* time consuming but it has been proved to be a valuable tool for success. Often there has only been one story written at great length. Looking for the things you *can* do, rather than those you *cannot*, soon becomes a habit.

Craig, aged 9, had a habit of calling out inappropriately in literacy, numeracy or any other discussion time and was usually in trouble for it by the end of the day. This was unfortunate because he often had interesting contributions. His teachers had tried to encourage appropriate behaviour by talking to him, rewarding him for not interrupting, punishing him for interrupting after three warnings. However, putting his hand up and waiting to be invited to speak, thus taking turns with others in his group, still did not come naturally.

Craig created a story called 'Charlie Chatterbox'. He did not want the book to be about himself. Craig started thinking of things that he could do to stop himself from breaking classroom rules, but still allowing him to contribute all that he wanted to the discussion. His first idea was to sit on his hands. He assured his Learning Support Assistant that he could do this without drawing attention to himself and so he wrote: 'Charlie loved science and did not want to be sent out of the lesson for interrupting. So as soon as this topic was introduced, Charlie sat on his hands. Every time he was able to answer a question, he pulled his hand out and put it up as high as he could'.

Craig found that this worked for him for a short while and then he would forget. He also found that it was far more difficult in Religious Education or English when he could express his own ideas at length. He decided to use his LSA as a 'filter' and when he wanted to say something, he whispered it to her first. This meant that he was able to release the words he was longing to say and got some immediate feedback. He wrote: 'Charlie decided that instead of shouting out, he would whisper to his friend'. Craig was asked why he used the word 'friend' rather than 'helper' or the person's name. He said that he was writing these ideas for other people who found it difficult not to shout out and anyway he did not want people to know that he had to have help. It was rather noisy and became rather disruptive, but it was important to try!

By the time Craig had finished his book (it took two weeks) he had entries like: 'Charlie said, "Instead of calling out I can count to four." Or "I could talk into a Dictaphone!"' In the end, Craig decided that while the others were contributing he would write his ideas down on a jotting pad, but as he was dyslexic the entries were usually unintelligible to anyone else. It did, however, satisfy his need to do something in response to the situation. Craig read his book at every opportunity in the day and his teacher would ask him which 'Chatterbox strategy' he was going to use before each discussion. The most important thing as far as the teacher was concerned was to enable him to shine at something he was good at, but not bulldoze all the other pupils out of the discussion. He was last seen when he was 11 years old and more often than not he was sitting on his hands. When asked about it, he explained that it was the discomfort that reminded him to put up his hand instead of calling out.

Neil was very aggressive in the playground and found it very difficult to get through 20 minutes without being sent inside. When questioned, he wanted a particular child to play with him and did not want to share his time with any other children. As a large 7-year-old he was quite intimidating and the staff had put into place some social communication games, such as Circle of Friends activities and a reward chart for every 5 minutes' of good behaviour at playtime.

It was decided to write a social story as part of his 'start the day' session and as a dyslexic child it was an opportunity to do some multisensory spelling work as well. He had difficulty thinking positively and he had to start by pretending his best 'friend' was away.

If Shaun was away . . .

- 'I could stand near the teacher and talk to her.'
- 'I could eat my snack then talk to the teacher.'
- 'I could run round the playground twice, eat my snack and stand near the teacher.'
- 'I could join in a game of skipping.'
- 'I could bring my football to school.'

Once he had the idea that he could do things on his own at playtime, he got quite inventive but it was necessary to run off some of his energy first and keep up the rewards. In Circle Time, Neil was given a chance to be on the 'hot spot'. This is an activity where each child can volunteer to say something that they like about the child on the 'hot spot' (or special chair). Neil's mother reported the next day that Neil was really pleased that the other children in his class had so much praise for his football ability. He never needed a social story again. He seemed to channel all his aggression into sports of different kinds.

Dyspraxia

Dyspraxia means a difficulty with the acquisition of patterns of movement. It can therefore affect speech and language, hand–eye coordination – especially handwriting – and organisation. The overlap of difficulties with those who are termed dyslexic is enormous. However, it is the child who has difficulty with handwriting – expressing himself on paper – and with physical activities rather than reading and spelling which determines the difference between dyslexia and dyspraxia. He may merely be termed 'clumsy' and receive little help or understanding of his needs. He, too, will tire easily and often become the butt of classroom jokes.

In the same way that there is a point at which a child with speech and language processing difficulties needs the specialist treatment of a speech and language therapist, so too there is the point at which a dyspraxic child needs the specialist attention of an occupational therapist or phys-iotherapist. As with dyslexia and ADD the remedial approach for dyspraxia may have to take into account many of the same strategies. In particular:

---

developing listening skills – Chapter 3, Speech and language processing

improving speech and articulation – Chapter 3, Speech and language processing

building self-esteem – Chapter 1, Dyslexia; Chapter 14, Summary

handwriting techniques – Chapter 8, Handwriting

organisation of himself, his belongings and his work – Chapter 13, Classroom management

---

Beyond these there will have to be specific exercises to improve balance, manipulation and coordination, perhaps incorporated into the gym lessons (Chapter 5, Movement). These exercises, when undertaken along with the teaching recommendations in this book, are well-proven to facilitate the learning process and enable children to build their basic skills on a firmer foundation.

Conclusions

As mentioned in Chapter 1, so often lines between diagnoses become blurred because children – and adults – are complex individuals. Other difficulties almost inevitably cloud any clear-cut diagnosis. This is certainly the case with diagnoses of ADD and dyspraxia where many of the recom-mendations for appropriate tuition and specialist remediation are similar to those recommended for dyslexic children. Perhaps, generally speaking, the simplest way of putting it is that it is:

1   the difficulty with words read, words spelt, words pronounced, words written and association of meanings with words which is essentially appropriate for a dyslexia diagnosis;
2   a difficulty with concentration, together with a tendency to impulsive behaviour (and in ADHD a tendency to hyperactivity) which is essen-tial for the ADD or ADHD label;
3   a difficulty with mastering patterns of movement and a tendency to clumsiness which makes a dyspraxic diagnosis appropriate; and

4   a difficulty with speech and language processing which is the basis of that diagnosis.

So many of the recommendations for classroom activities overlap with all these diagnoses that in the end – with differentiation – they become *good teaching practice*. Many appropriate recommendations for ADD, dyspraxia and a speech and language problem are, therefore, to be found within all chapters.

Chapter 5

Movement

'It seems bizarre to me, doing some exercises and expecting that to help him learn his spellings', said one mother after an interview with the school Special Educational Needs Coordinator. Yet, it has been proved that movement in the form of exercises can help children to learn, and more and more schools are incorporating them into the daily curriculum.

Dyslexia is a cognitive disorder – one that is part of our genetic make-up, so can only be helped rather than cured. New research is constantly being carried out to consider ways in which physical exercise can help dyslexic children and adults on a day-to-day basis.

Reflexes

Movement is the way a child gains control over his body. First, a baby in the womb develops primitive reflexes. These are automatic, involuntary responses needed for the birth process, survival and development in the first weeks of life. These have a limited life span and need to be replaced by more sophisticated reflexes to give a child increased control over balance and voluntary movement. If these primitive reflexes remain after 6–12 months they may prevent the development of later skills needed for reading and writing. How does a baby move on from the primitive reflex stage? Generally, through movement – any of the typical movements that a baby makes in the first year of his life, including kicking, rolling, sitting and crawling. Brain researchers tell us that gradually as we learn new skills, we develop concentration. Roughly, we can concentrate for as many minutes as we are years of age! By the age of 7–8 years of age a child has usually developed a sense of balance as well as some degree of concentration. However, there are some children who are late in completing this development, who simply cannot keep still. A child needs to have control over his body before he can sit still on a chair and concentrate on reading and writing. Children instinctively know when they need more practice to establish control. Instead of telling these children to 'sit down' and 'sit still' we could allow them to stand and turn round quickly in either direction for 30 seconds. Researchers have shown that a child can then concentrate for a lot longer afterwards. Sadly, it is often the child who most needs to release the tension by moving who is the one that risks being kept in as a punishment.

Motor development

Dr Peter Blythe, at the Institute of Neuro-Physiological Psychology in Chester, UK, set out to search for a physical basis to learning difficulties. This research has led to a new way of thinking for many teachers and, as a result, many are starting to ask the question, 'Is this child physically and neurologically ready to learn?'.

Children above the age of 7–8 years who show a cluster of the following problems:

- travel sickness;
- difficulty learning to ride a two-wheeled bicycle;
- PE difficulties;
- difficulty learning to swim;
- poor hand–eye coordination;
- difficulty learning to read;
- difficulty in learning to write;
- difficulty in making the transition from printing to cursive script;
- difficulty in learning to tell the time;
- mixed laterality;
- unable to sit still;
- speech and articulation difficulties,

may benefit from a simple movement programme, devised by a qualified neuro-developmental therapist. This can be done via the doctor, but it may be a good idea to make contact with one of the addresses given at the end of the book. The Special Educational Needs Coordinator (SENCO) at school can refer a child, via the school Medical Officer, to the local Occupational Therapy Department. Problems can be identified and pro-grammes devised to be carried out at school or at home. These programmes need to be carried out daily for 5–10 minutes.

Normal motor development occurs from head to toe, then from the trunk outwards. If you imagine an invisible line down the centre of your body and call it the 'midline', the next developments are movements either side of this midline. For example, a child will pick up something on the right-hand side of the table, with his right hand, pass it to his left hand and place it on the left side of the table. Lastly, movement across the midline ensures complete coordination; so the child will pick something up on his right-hand side and, stretching across his body, place it down on the left. By the age of seven years children should be fully integrated, with both sides of the brain and body working together. It is not coincidence that it is at this age we see many children take off with their reading. Much of a child's development happens through natural play activities.

Playing games

This generation's experience of 'play' is very different from that of preceding generations. Computer-generated games, TV, video, DVD entertainment and constant use of the car, have all too often cut out the exercise patterns of previous years. Many gymnastic activities, such as rope climbing, vaulting over the 'horse' or 'box' have been postponed until the health and safety rules can be followed to the letter of the law. Too many teachers are worried about lawsuits to flout the rules these days. Safety issues for children as they play outside curtail such a lot of good movement development. Cycling, walking, tree climbing have all to be organised so that the parents know exactly where their children are. How depressing this all sounds, but teachers can do a great deal to remediate this sad situation by encouraging playground games and field activities that include climbing, crawling, rolling, spinning and balancing. Take children near a slope and they will want to roll down it. Walk along the road and they will want to climb onto the neighbour's wall, balancing instinctively as they go. These games are a normal part of child development, but some children need more opportunities for these activities (known as vestibular stimulation) than others.

Movement of any kind stimulates a 'feel good' factor in human beings. Children who spend all day on a computer must unwittingly miss out on so much basic social training. Perhaps because the value of games is underestimated, some of the knock-on benefits such as co-operation, turn taking and fairness have been lost. Teachers may be relying on Circle Time and PSE (Personal, Social Education) to inculcate such things as following rules and not cheating, caring and sharing or developing friendships, but group games can create an ethos in which friendships develop naturally. In fact, the more games a youngster knows the more popular he tends to be. Children have to learn to take responsibility for their own actions when playing with others; competition – learning to lose, as well as the enjoyment of winning – is a rehearsal for life. Some children are helped by the support that games give in developing and maintaining friendships; perhaps even with someone they had previously felt to be daunting. The disapproval of their peers, if they are discovered cheating, can lead to natural retribution, as they are ostracised. Bullies prefer solitary victims so those who play games with others are less likely to be bullied. These are some of the observations of Cat Weatherill in her book, *Primary Playground Games*.

In the 1970s the dyslexia specialist would have done very practical activities, for example, listening to and recognising the different noises outside the classroom for sound discrimination or throwing and catching balls for hand–eye coordination but, as time went on, dyslexia teaching tended to be in cramped spaces so the pencil and paper exercises rather took over and the physical activities were eclipsed. Now it is realised that exercises that mimic the natural development of babies and toddlers are very important and enable not only children, but also adults, to acquire literacy and numeracy techniques much more rapidly.

Movement to learn

Barbara Pheloung in Sydney, NSW has done a considerable amount of work in this field. Apart from the books she has written – *Help Your Child to Learn* and *Help Your Class to Learn* – she has devised motor programmes that can enable children – and adults – to be ready to learn. She has recently made available a DVD and a video entitled 'Movement to Learn' which, when used with her books, comprehensively illustrates the programmes. She claims, 'You only need a few minutes daily to change a child.' These minutes can be incorporated into the school day at some convenient time, maybe first thing in the morning or a break time. *It must be noted that these exercises should be done on PE mats or smooth floors rather than a carpet as the friction generated can result in 'carpet burn'.*

'Flip flops' is an exercise that is recommended as a daily activity, for nine months to a year if at all possible. Flip flops are best learnt in three stages and then gradually joined into one continuous, flowing movement.

There are two variants of this exercise but start with unilateral flip flops (see page 45).

Once this is mastered try cross-patterned flip flops (see page 46).

Unilateral stomach sliding/commando crawling is also a valuable exercise (see page 47).

Once secure try cross-pattern stomach sliding/commando crawling (see page 47).

The last of these movement exercises is crawling (unilateral and cross-pattern crawling see page 48). So often a child with poor handwriting has been a 'bottom shuffler' or has simply gone from sitting to walking without the essential hand–eye coordination training which comes so easily from crawling.

These illustrations are based on those used in Barbara Pheloung's book entitled *Help Your Class to Learn* and used with her permission.

Unilateral flip flops

Figure (a) demonstrates the starting position: child lies on stomach, head turned to the right, looking at the right thumb. The right leg is bent at right angles at the knee. The left hand and arm are down by the side and the left leg is down straight.

(a)

(b)

Figure (b) shows what happens as the child says, 'Down one', as right arm and leg go slowly down to the side together.

Figure (c) Child says, 'Head one', as head turns to look to the left.

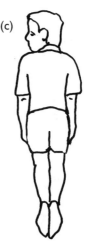
(c)

Figure (d) is the finish position. The child says, 'Up one', as the left leg and arm are slowly moved to the position that the right arm and leg had, with eyes looking at the left thumb.

(d)

The child now continues with, 'Down two', 'Head two', 'Up two', etc. for the agreed number of times. Start with six and gradually increase but make sure that as much of their body as possible keeps in contact with the floor and the head, arm and leg arrive in their destination at the same time.

Cross-patterned flip flops

Begin with the head turned to the right, right
arm bent with the thumb across from the
eyes.

(e)

Figure (e) this time the left leg is bent while
the right leg is straight. The left hand is placed
in the small of the back.

(f)

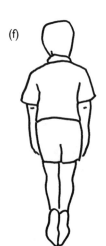

Figure (f) shows, 'Down
one'.

(g)

Figure (g) shows, 'Head one'.

(h)

Figure (h)
demonstrates the
finish position after,
'Up one'.

Again, start with six and gradually increase
in both number and speed.

Unilateral stomach sliding/commando crawl

This starts in the same position as for the unilateral flip flops, but the child slides forward with each change by pressing down with his hand and digging in with the toe of his bent leg as it straightens.

(i)   (j)

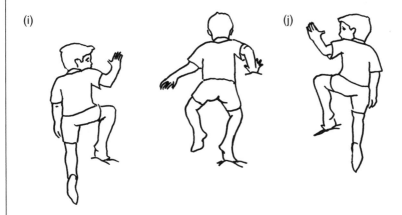

The child may need help to keep the arm and the leg not only moving together but also completing the movement at the same time.

Cross-pattern stomach sliding/commando crawl

Start with the cross-pattern flip flop position and use the sliding movements as in the unilateral commando crawl. The child may find it difficult to move the opposite arm and leg absolutely together. It can help if the adult can count with him.

(k)   (l)

Unilateral crawling

Child starts on hands and knees, like a dog, with hands and knees shoulder width apart. The right knee and right hand move together and hit the floor at the same time. The fingers of the hand point straight ahead with the thumb pointing inwards. The knees are lifted while the feet and the toes are dragged along the floor. The head turns and eyes look at each hand in

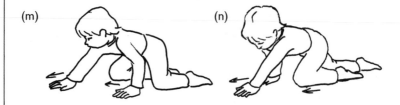

the forward position. If the child cannot do all these together at first, start with what he can do and gradually add the rest.

Cross-pattern crawling

This is the same activity except that in cross-crawling the opposite arms and legs move together.

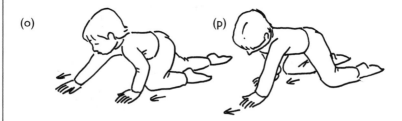

Brain Gym

Many schools in the UK are starting the day with a movement class based on either these exercises or Brain Gym activities, which help the nervous system to work more efficiently. These exercises can improve the ability to listen more carefully and enable a child to function more effectively. The work of Dr Paul Dennison and Gail Dennison has provided a series of good classroom activities, derived from their book *Edu K for Kids*, that can make the difference between a child switching off or remaining alert.

The following activities are some favourites that have been tried by classroom teachers and found to work.

Drinking water improves energy and concentration and it should be made available for those who need it. Still water can be provided in sports bottles and kept in a convenient place. Many teachers are nervous that it will be a gimmick that some children may take advantage of, but experience shows that most children settle to only asking when it is needed. Teachers will soon become aware of those children. The brain assimilates water drunk at room temperature more readily than chilled water. Although tea, coffee and squash are made with water, the tongue sends the message to the brain that this is food, not water and the stomach starts the digestive process. The same happens with carbonated water, so teachers need to be strict if children are allowed to bring their own drinks. Still water only! Children who need copious amounts of water very rarely need to keep visiting the toilet. They need it to restore energy and concentration. Water makes up about 70 per cent of our bodies so it is important to maintain hydration.

When a task involves listening, reading, writing or spelling, or the whole class seems restless, a good exercise is the 'cross crawl' or cross-pattern marching. This can be done without fuss by standing up wherever they are. This is also good when a task requires a child to 'do' as well as think, as in science experiments or problem-solving activities in maths.

Cross-crawl is done very slowly (hence the name). Standing, you touch your right hand to the left knee, which is raised, as if you are marching slowly on the spot. Then the left hand swings across to the right knee and so on. This needs to be done alternately 10–25 times quite slowly (Fig. 1). You can also do this sitting down.

Fig. 1

Marching is a good exercise in its own right. It helps to highlight the children who may have difficulty with spelling and writing because they have not yet integrated the two sides of their body to work together. These are the children whose right arm swings with their right leg and their left arm with their left leg. With daily 'cross-crawl' practice they begin to use both sides of their brain to do the tasks that some children appear to do quite naturally.

'Lazy eights' is an appropriate exercise for children who find reversals, and handwriting in general, a problem. It also helps a child to track accurately when reading and may be fitted in at odd times of the school day. It is most successfully done at a large whiteboard so the teacher can mark the spot where the child's eyes focus. That point is the mid point of the infinity symbol ∞, or an eight lying on its side being lazy. With the arm extended straight out in front, the child draws the symbol beginning upwards – in either direction. The movement needs to be free flowing, but the head must remain still so that the eyes can follow the movement of the hand. It does not matter how big it is, but the peripheral range of the eyes will limit it. Start by doing it three times with each hand and then three times with both hands clasped together. Once a child can do this smoothly extend the activity by stretching the arm out with the thumb pointing upwards. Make the lazy eight movements and check that the

Fig. 2

child's head remains still and his eyes follow the movements accurately (Fig. 2). He can then do the activity himself but the teacher needs to ensure that as he draws the 8, he starts tracking at eye-level. Once secure, this can be done with a whole group of children.

A further activity can be drawn out of this exercise such as 'alphabet eights' and these can be done on the classroom whiteboard. Start drawing the lazy eights and then call out 'd'. The child has to use the framework of the infinity symbol to find how to form the letter 'd' smoothly. 'What about b?' Each letter of the alphabet can be explored creatively but 'b' and 'd' are especially worthwhile because of the over-learning of the visual image that takes place, as well as identifying the feeling that is involved in forming these two letters which are so often confused (Fig. 3).

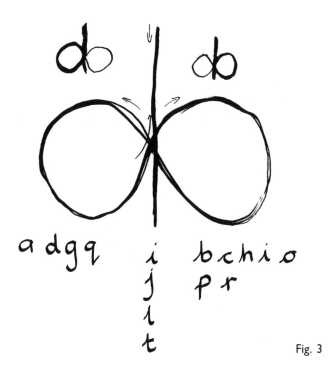

Fig. 3

Conclusion

In conclusion, many schools are already using movement programmes and making time to incorporate them into the school day. Sometimes it is the class teacher that identifies the child who is in need of these developmental exercises, sometimes it is the SENCO, Teacher's Assistant or parent, but however the child is identified, it is important to include some kind of movement programme into any portfolio of ideas for target setting. A child with a specific learning difficulty needs to have the chance to ensure the foundations for learning are secure and ready for use.

Chapter 6

Reading

Difficulties with reading are often the first point at which a child is recognised as having particular needs in his teaching. Success or failure in this area is extremely emotive. There is little else so anxiety-provoking to parents as when their child seems stuck, while his peers advance with apparent ease through the levels of a reading scheme. Those who learn to read with little effort start their school careers with a distinct advantage in today's society.

Intellectual grasp of facts, logic, reasoning, imagination, lateral thinking and creative skills may all be present to a very high degree, even though a child seems unable to cope adequately with the written word. The emphasis on the acquisition of literacy skills all too often leaves a child bearing the burden of feeling that he is, in fact, stupid and inadequate. The deplorable effect of the subsequent erosion of confidence cannot be stressed too strongly.

It is always important to ascertain that there is no physiological reason for a reading difficulty and that appropriate checks have been carried out (see Chapter 2, Ears, eyes and IQs).

Reading is part of the total language process and, therefore, it is not surprising that a child who has had early difficulties with speech and language may subsequently struggle with reading. Late speech, immature sentence structure, confusion between similar sounds and words, with a possible history of glue ear (see Chapter 2, Ears, eyes and IQs) are all warning signs that there may be the need for specific help with reading. However, there are also children who are extremely articulate, with a good and extensive vocabulary, but who nevertheless experience enormous difficulty when faced with the written word.

Reading difficulties may manifest themselves initially with the actual mechanics of reading but, even if these are mastered, there may be problems with comprehension. It is not unusual for a child to attain a reasonable level of accuracy in decoding words and to continue to have difficulty in extracting the meaning from the text, perhaps because his concentration is centred on the phonological process.

A reasonable reading speed, as well as accuracy, is also essential for coping adequately with the demands of the school curriculum, and especially, for instance, when under pressure in examinations. Even minor inaccuracies may have major consequences; for instance, the omission of the word 'not' when reading examination questions.

Tests

Reading tests and their scores need careful consideration. There may be a considerable discrepancy between the scores achieved on a graded word test such as Vernon or Schonell and one of narrative form such as New Neale or New Macmillan where contextual clues are relevant (NFER Nelson). Reading test results are therefore useful as a yardstick or indicator but should not be taken as a hard and fast figure, and ought to be considered as one more small piece of information which goes to make up the whole picture. Also, a child's score on one day may be different from that on another, especially if he is having an off-day. Sometimes a teacher *knows* a child has made progress, but this progress is not reflected in his reading score.

All reading tests should be used diagnostically, for the way in which a child tackles the tests gives useful indications of his areas of strength and weakness. Often, time only allows for general screening tests in class, but individual diagnostic testing is vital for the child who appears to be failing. This information can give pointers to the type of problems a child may be experiencing and may also prove a useful reference at a later stage for another teacher.

General class screening tests need to be studied carefully. A match in reading age and chronological age does not necessarily rule out a reading problem. A bright child should be capable of scoring a reading age even two years ahead of the standardised average for his chronological age. The criterion to be looked at should always be the discrepancy between performance and the potential to satisfy his intellectual needs.

Analysis

As has already been said, literacy skills require good visual recall for words, good phonological skills (auditory recall for letter-sounds) and kinaesthetic strengths (strengths developed through movements and feel in the muscles). These skills make for fluency in spelling and handwriting. If there are weaknesses in these areas, literacy difficulties will follow.

A teacher should look at the ways in which a child tackles reading:

- Is he confident, relaxed, anxious, fidgety or unwilling?
- Does he rely on pictures and contextual clues?

- Has he memorised the text from a previous occasion or from hearing others in the class read the same passage? This may mislead a class teacher into believing that a child can read.
- Does he really recognise a word on a flash card or is it, for instance, the torn corner, ink spot or initial letter that is giving him the necessary clue?

Children are often extremely clever at pretending to master basic skills rather than allowing their failure to do so to become apparent. Some learn that as long as they keep talking and the gist is right, the teacher may not have her full attention on their page and they can slide over the difficult bits. This happens in classrooms where an overstretched teacher may be hearing two children read at once and is also attempting to explain something or spell a word to yet another.

Miscue analysis

When a child reads, what type of errors does he make?

- Does he look at the initial letter and guess wildly?
- Does he find it difficult to keep his place on the line?
- Does he omit words, add words, substitute something similar either in look or meaning (**collapse/capsize**), confuse certain letters (**b/d, u/n, p/g, t/f** and so on), confuse little words (**of/for/from**), reverse words (**was/saw**), foreshorten words (**rember/remember**), or add extra syllables?
- Can he read consistently in a left to right direction?
- Does he give attention to, or ignore, punctuation?
- Is there expression?
- Finally, most important of all, has he understood what he has read?

This analysis may be done informally or formally. The child is given the text to read while the teacher marks a parallel text, or the child reads into a tape recorder and the teacher subsequently marks the actual text. The types of errors made give useful clues to the nature of the difficulties and how to rectify them.

The following passage was read by Mark, a very bright 7½ year old. The reading was very hesitant and he used his finger to keep his place on the line; he had already had his eyes fully checked:

This is the Glen of Gloom. There are no g..r..green (sounding out) **plants in the** (substitution) **glen. There are no g..ar..gar..garden** (sounding out) **flows** (pronounced 'floes' – mispronunciation and omission); **just twigs** (substitution), **trees, brown weeds and some**

c..l..u..s..t.. cl..us..ters.. clusters (sounding out) of o..r..a..ng.. orang (sounding out and mispronunciation) **and yellow mushroom** (omission) **sticking up for** (substitution) **the map.. mub.. mud** (substitution and reversal) **and clay. Animals need** (substitution) **stay** (omission) **into the Glen of Gloom.**

The correct version:

This is the Glen of Gloom. There are no green plants in this glen. There are no garden flowers; just twisty trees, brown weeds and some clusters of orange and yellow mushrooms sticking up from the mud and clay. Animals never stray into the Glen of Gloom.
(Colin Harris, *The Glen of Gloom* (1984), by kind permission of Oxford University Press)

Alex, aged 10 years 1 month, had a reading accuracy of 8 years 1 month. She is very bright and seen as a good communicator so was not considered to have any significant problem at school although she appeared to have slight word-finding difficulties and some minor grammatical immaturities. An assessment from a speech and language therapist states, **'Alex is unlikely to appear to the untrained observer as a child with speech and language difficulties. However she does experience some specific difficulties which are not in line with her developed abilities in other areas.'**
She is inclined to attack the reading with little regard to the sense, as can be seen in this example:

As the mountains (substitution) **climbed the steep** (omission) **point of the bridge,** (substitution) **the wind changed** (omission) **the tempera-ture dropped. After a little white** (substitution) **snowflakes began to fall and vis.. in.. invisible** (substitution) **was reducked** (soft C not recognised) **to a few yards. They knew** (omission) **they must descent** (substitution or mispronunciation) **rapidly but at the same time caution was needed. They could magic** (substitution) **their com.. com.. comp** (refusal) **wanting** (substitution) **anxiously at the camp on the p.. pl.. plat.. platyou** (mispronunciation) **below. Suddenly there was a distinct** (substitution) **rumble as they peered thought** (substitution) **the swilling** (substitution) **snowflakes wandering** (substitution) **where the safest rout** (substitution or mispronunciation) **lay.**

The correct version:

As the mountaineers climbed the steepest point of the ridge, the wind changed and the temperature dropped. After a little while, snowflakes began to fall and visibility was reduced to a few yards. They knew that they must descend rapidly but that at the same time caution was needed. They could imagine their companions waiting anxiously at the camp on the plateau below. Suddenly there was a distant rumble as they peered through the swirling snowflakes wondering where the safest route lay.

William, aged 15, had a reading age of 10 years 6 months. He read:

Charles (substitution) **steered into a small inlet in the island. The weary paddles** (omission) **gave a sign** (substitution) **of relief after three hours of battling with the fierce current. One by one they clambered on** (addition) **to the shore and searched** (substitution) **themselves.**

'Two of the four-men (substitution) **tents will do. I'll** (omission) **be a crush but we'll manage. You'll be glad for** (substitution) **the sleeping bags. It gets very cold at night.'**

The correct version:

Carlsen steered into a small inlet in the island. The weary paddlers gave a sigh of relief after three hours of battling with the fierce current. One by one they clambered to the shore and stretched themselves. 'Two of the four-man tents will do. It'll be a crush but we'll manage. You'll be glad of the sleeping bags. It gets very cold at night.'
(Arthur J. Evans, *Reading and Thinking* (1987), by kind permission of Learning Materials Ltd)

William was into his GCSE course and faced with English, Maths, Science, German, Sports Science, Geography and Geology. His set book was *Catcher in the Rye*. Sports Science, Geography and Geology were subjects full of specialist vocabulary. Despite an IQ assessment placing him in the top 10 per cent of the population, his results would prove to be a poor reflection of both his potential and his efforts.

At 7 years 6 months Mark's reading had made progress and there were many children of his age who were not even at this level, and Alex (10 years 1 month) could read well enough to manage in school. However, without the right sort of help the gap between their reading age and their academic needs could only widen. They would then be in the same predicament as William.

Reading develops in three stages:

- Recognition and recall of the letter shapes.
- Linkage of these shapes to sounds/words.
- Shapes and sounds are invested with meaning.

Initially, the teacher must ascertain which of these stages the child has reached. Having assessed the child's level of performance and specific areas of strength or weakness, it is necessary to consider the teaching methods being used and adapt them accordingly. Real Books, Look-Say and Phonics all have their advocates and all have their successes. Jean Augur, former Director of Education at the British Dyslexia Association and with many years of experience, used to say that 'children fall into four categories':

- Those who learn to read with any method used.
- Those who, with time, adapt to any method used.
- Those who survive in spite of the method used.
- Those who sink *because* of the method used.

If a child is failing he will need a totally different approach from the one so far used. Appropriate methods for the individual are very important. A different strategy should be applied to teaching those *starting* to read and to those whose reading is inefficient. Some teenagers fall into both of these categories, and methods and materials must be geared to their age and interests (see Older children, page 61).

Special Needs teachers are constantly reminded to use a *structured, cumulative and multisensory* method. This means that they should adopt a simple, basic, step-by-step approach when dealing with areas of failure. As with all good teaching practice, everything that is taught links back to something already known. For instance, for those beginning to read, this would be the spoken word.

A multisensory approach is necessary to overcome and to compensate for weaknesses while building on strengths. Such an approach has the advantage of reinforcement from several learning channels at once. For example, the child is taught to listen to words. He should look closely at them and notice the shape of the word, and perhaps find little words that he already knows within the word (see Chapter 7, Spelling). He then links the spoken word to this visual image. He learns to sound out the word, having initially established letter/sound relationships. The word can be related to others similar in shape and/or sound. He writes each word and finally reads it. In this process *he has used his ears, his eyes, his speech and his hand* to use auditory, visual and kinaesthetic senses together. Neither pure phonics nor Look-Say are adequate for his needs. The use of colour, pictograms and word families lends further support to the senses, and hence to the memory.

Listening skills may be very poor in a child with a short concentration span. Many children lead lives which compete with a constant barrage of background noise, both at home and at school. The TV, traffic noise and other people's talking are a constant factor and, as so much of it is irrelevant to them, children learn to switch off. At the same time they also tire easily because of the strain of making a continual effort to distinguish those things which are important from those that are irrelevant.

The visual recall of some people may be very weak, even for pictures and objects. Others may be able to recall pictures and objects with ease, but are completely floored when they are faced with written symbols, both words and numbers. These are the children and adults whose visual recall for words is so poor that they can be told a word on one page and look at the same word on the next page – or even on the next line – and be unable to recognise it. They stare at the word as though they have never seen it before. This is especially irritating for a teacher or parent who does not understand the problem. But it must be realised that it is even more irritating and frustrating for the poor reader, who equally does not understand his own problem. These are the people who usually learn to read through learning to word-build or spell (see Chapter 7, Spelling).

Suggestions for teaching

Many of the following suggestions are practised by teachers of younger children, but the children we are describing will need more than the average amount of time and effort invested in them by their teachers. These children may be found in junior schools, still unable to read adequately. Moreover, many older children, even in secondary schools and who have slipped through the net, will still need reinforcement in these areas:

1   Children with poor language skills need:
    a   to be encouraged to describe events accurately and in sequence;
    b   to look at pictures and discuss what they see and be able to spec-
        ulate as to what has just happened or might happen next;
    c   to learn to sit still and listen to stories, or their peers recounting
        events (see Chapter 3, Speech and language processing).

2   Listening games, such as identifying common household noises from
    a tape, e.g. filling the kettle, telephone ringing, dog barking, etc.

3   Tell a simple story and ask the children to insert an appropriate word
    whenever you pause, which is, in effect, a spoken Cloze Procedure.
    (Cloze Procedure is a form of reading and comprehension exercise in
    which certain words have been omitted from the text and have to be
    re-inserted by the pupil.)

4   Teach children to tap or clap simple rhythms.

5   Find rhyming words or syllables.

6 Discriminate between or find words that have common beginnings, endings or vowel sounds, or pick the odd one out.

e.g. **tip**, **tap**, bat, **tub**
ten, pen, yet, men
bun, jam, **fun**, **sun**

7 Blending games such as g-oa-t – what is it?
It is important to use pure sounds and avoid the schwa (unstressed vowel) sound on the end of consonants. Work on blending becomes very difficult if instead of m-a-t the child is saying **mu-a-ter**.

8 Classifying objects or words.

9 Games of matching and recognising shapes and jigsaw puzzles.

10 Memory games, with additional discussion on the details of differences in similar objects; e.g. whether the button has two holes or four, its colour, etc.

11 Tracking materials such as those produced by Ann Arbor. These strengthen the left to right direction of reading and also include sequencing (see Chapter 2, Ears, eyes and IQs and Chapter 9, Sequencing).

12 Books of visual discrimination exercises are available. A teacher may make her own sets of exercises, initially with pictures:

and then leading on to individual letters,

b	b	d	p	q	b	d

digraphs,

ai	ia	ai	oi	io	ai	ia

and, in time, digraphs within words, progressing to the next stage as each level is mastered,

| road | read | raid | road | rood | raid | road |

and so on.

As children develop the ability to recognise specific shapes, so these are also linked to the sound.

13   When both auditory and visual recall are weak, children may learn better through tactile and kinaesthetic work. Letters can be traced in sand or on sandpaper, or made with plasticine, Blu-Tack or Playdoh.

14   Large tracing movements of letter-shapes can be made in the air or on a board or large sheets of newspaper so that there is gross muscular movement. As confidence increases, children can practise this with eyes closed. It is extremely important that the formation should be executed correctly, and so this should be carefully supervised (see Chapter 8, Handwriting). It is another opportunity to form a link if the correct letter-sound is said aloud as the letter-shape is being traced.

Some of these suggestions sound rather basic for a teenager or adult but are acceptable if suitably presented. Although this may be considered the province of the Special Needs Department, class teachers need to be aware of the various strategies to improve reading.

Once a child has mastered even a few of the letter-sound associations he has the tools to begin tackling unfamiliar words. He can begin to analyse and synthesise and then decode the printed word. At this stage he begins to understand that there is a reason for choosing particular letters and putting them in a certain order.

Various schemes used by specialist teachers recommend a specific order in which to teach first the letters and then the blends. The Edith Norrie Letter-Case, the Hickey Multi-Sensory Language Course, Letterland (Pictogram), Gill Cotterell's Phonic Reference Cards, Alpha to Omega, TRTS (Teaching Reading through Spelling), the Bangor Dyslexia Teaching System and, in recent years, THRASS (Teaching Handwriting, Reading and Spelling Skills), all set out a structured approach. THRASS, devised in the UK by Davies and Ritchie, is primarily for class teaching, but is also suitable for dyslexic children who need to progress at a slower rate with much reinforcement. The scheme includes activity sheets and computer programs.

The National Literacy Strategy which has been developed for use in primary schools in the UK is an attempt to raise standards of reading, spelling and grammar. There is no doubt that the scheme is extremely comprehensive and useful. However, there is a great deal for teachers to get through in the daily hour assigned to literacy and children with problems in this area often need extra support if they are to keep up. If possible, for a dyslexic child who is needing immediate help with a concern, it is better to deal with that problem straightaway, rather than stick to a rigid system.

If a child is failing, it may be wise to discard the reading scheme being used by the school. Structured schemes generally give a better base from which to work than picking books at random or choosing for interest alone (Real Books approach). Ideally, libraries for infants should have a wide range of initial reading schemes, so that, for example, a child with poor visual memory but an awareness of sounds can make progress along with his peers; a spelling road to reading is often the best approach, particularly for a non-starter, for a time discarding reading books altogether (see Chapter 7, Spelling). Fluent reading, with good comprehension, is better achieved by encouraging a child to read books which interest him; pressurising and pushing a child on to the next grade should be resisted. He may cope with the mechanics but *must also be able to comprehend* what he has read. Motivation is far better when the demands are not too high and the child can actually enjoy reading. Unfortunately, many reading schemes seem to make a sudden jump in difficulty level. Some stories with content for younger children have complicated sentence structure, which may need explanation. Consideration of size and clarity of print is also important.

In early stages, reading books with rhythm and rhyme, such as some of the Dr Seuss books, help to develop fluency. Likewise, some children find it very helpful to re-read familiar texts.

Older children

Once a child has the tools to tackle words by sequencing the correct sounds, he will be ready to move on to more complex words. Here again, learning to read through understanding word structure enables the child to comprehend syllable division, progressing to root words, prefixes, suffixes and compound words (see pages 83–4).

Some, although they may feel it is a babyish habit, need encouragement to use their finger as a pointer beneath the words, not in order to anchor their eyes because of an eye problem, but because it improves fluency and comprehension. Some teachers feel that fluency can be impaired by using a finger, but it is often helpful to those who have struggled and may have a residual weakness – especially when tired and under pressure (see Chapter 2, Ears, eyes and IQs). A marker, a card or ruler to keep the eye on the line is better used above the line being read rather than below, where it masks what is to come and consequently restricts natural eye movement for the words ahead.

Cloze Procedure gives a good indication of whether or not the child is able to read and comprehend the text. Periodically, as he reads, the child should be asked to tell the story to the teacher without referring to the text. He should also be encouraged to predict the possible events and outcome of the story.

Older children may well have mastered the basic skills and score reasonably on a reading test, particularly as these use familiar vocabulary. However, their rate of reading and ability to extract meaning falls when they are faced with unexpected or unknown words. For instance, the vocabularies for subjects such as Physics and Chemistry are not easy, and reading skills are more than put to the test when the text appears to be a foreign language. These children need clearly presented information in their textbooks with good support from headings, sub-headings, illustrations and diagrams.

Secondary school subject teachers should be aware that extra time may be needed for a pupil to complete reading assignments just as much as for written ones. Different reading skills are needed for different purposes, such as skimming (see Chapter 12, Study skills).

Parental involvement

Parents of young children often become more involved with their reading than with any other part of the school curriculum, and good communication between teacher and parent can save much heartache. Children are very quick to pick up the anxieties of their parents, so that even positive support can be a form of pressure to some who are particularly keen to please and not disappoint a loved parent. Parents should be fully informed of the nature of any difficulties and the strategies being used to overcome them. Many of the visual and auditory recognition exercises can be done in the form of games and are an acceptable form of homework, but should only be done if it is a pleasure for both child and parent. If there is any anxiety on the parent's part or resentment on the part of the child, it should be stopped immediately; otherwise a class or special needs teacher will have the extra job of undoing the resentment that has built up before the child is able to learn.

Nevertheless, anxious parents do want to help their children. When home-reading sessions have become stressful, parents may have an acute sense of failure and this is not helped by being advised to *leave it to the school*. They need to be given something positive to do. In cases where there is such anxiety or in the early stages, reading practice at home may be inappropriate. *There is, though, immense value to be gained by parents reading to their children.* Listening skills, language development, expansion of vocabulary and general knowledge are all augmented. Books also become accepted as a source of information and pleasure rather than of distress and failure. Some parents have, themselves, experienced reading difficulties and may prefer to listen with the child to some of the many good story tapes that are now available at local libraries. This has the added advantage, when appropriate, of providing a book for following the text at the same time.

Paired reading

A number of teachers and chartered educational psychologists suggest that a child might be helped at home by paired reading. This is a scheme with recommended instructions, but any one of the following may be useful:

1 The parent reads, with the child joining in as and when he can.
2 Read alternate paragraphs/pages/chapters.
3 The child reads, but the parent supplies a word as soon as he gets stuck and allows the odd inaccuracy providing it does not change the sense. In this way fluency and interest are not continually interrupted.

Some children do take off, but it is important that parents realise that this may be a long-term problem and a few weeks' boost will not necessarily overcome all difficulties. Unfortunately, some parents find they are bombarded by conflicting *good* advice from a variety of sources, leaving them yet more confused and anxious.

Reading Recovery

Much publicity was given to the Reading Recovery programme instigated in New Zealand by Marie Clay. Undoubtedly, many children benefit enormously from the daily individual session for this relatively short time and make pleasing progress. Some teachers still use this effectively.

There are a number of children who will continue to need support throughout their schooling. However, some of these, through the progress they have made with reading, are not then recognised as needing support with the written word. Too often teachers have said of a child, 'He can't be dyslexic – he can read quite well'. These are the children who perhaps do not appear to be failing until they are at least 8 years old. They have managed to cope with a basic sight vocabulary. Such children in independent schools may already be in classes where they are going to be under considerable pressure because they gained places on the strength of a reading test taken at the age of 6 or 7. Furthermore, it may have been a test that concentrated on the mechanics of reading – that is, decoding – and when reading in context they fail to understand because all their attention has to be given to recognition of the letter-content of words and their memory of what they have already read fails them.

Adults

Because many class teachers are also adult literacy teachers, they are no doubt aware that adults need recognition of the courage that it has taken for them to admit to needing help. To be faced with childish reading materials and apparatus that they link with previous failure is of course counter-productive. Although they will also need tuition in the basic language structure, initial stages may be built around words commonly used on public notices: for example, **stop, open, danger, entry, exit, closed,** as well as a person's address and addresses of family members. Later, expediency usually demands that the emphasis is linked to the particular needs of the individual and his employment. Form-filling, stock-ordering, cheques and invoice words may be his priority, and help should be along these lines rather than a rigid, pre-determined remedial programme. Attention might need to be given to interpretation of bus and train time-tables. Abbreviations in advertisements may be a total enigma. What possible interpretation could be given to **HGV driver reqd**?

Conclusions

Even when the basic skill has been mastered, many dyslexic children continue to read slowly, even into adulthood. Furthermore, they often need to re-read a text for full comprehension. Given appropriate teaching, encouragement and time, they can make good progress, although some will never do more than read for information or necessity. Others even become enthusiastic, and it is always rewarding to see a child who has struggled initially turn to reading for pleasure.

Chapter 7

Spelling

Although reading has always been given more prominence than spelling in the early days at school, spelling, in fact, poses the greater problem for dyslexic children, and this difficulty can continue long after the reading difficulty has been greatly improved. Poor spelling is usually a lifetime's embarrassment.

Any difficulty with reading is given early attention because the ability to read unlocks the door to so much information both in and out of school. In the past, children have been told that the more they read the better they will be able to spell. But for many people this is just not true. In fact, spelling is a totally different skill using different neurological pathways. A woman, 45 years old, coming for spelling lessons once said that she had been reading for forty years and was still unable to write many words correctly.

There are people who have no visual recall for words (they may visualise in pictures or see nothing in their mind's eye), but when confronted with words, the sight of them sparks off the recognition, and they may read fluently. (For those of us who cannot visualise in pictures, this can be compared with an inability to picture a person clearly in the mind, but we recognise that person when we see him.) Many times this reading ability has led to a wrong conclusion about a child not being dyslexic, with the suggestion that poor spelling was mere laziness or his mind working too fast to allow him to give proper attention to his work. Teachers often describe this as **his brain working too quickly for his hand**.

Tim, aged 16, with a Full Scale IQ of 134, reads fluently. As can be seen in Example A, his writing is almost illegible:

Example A

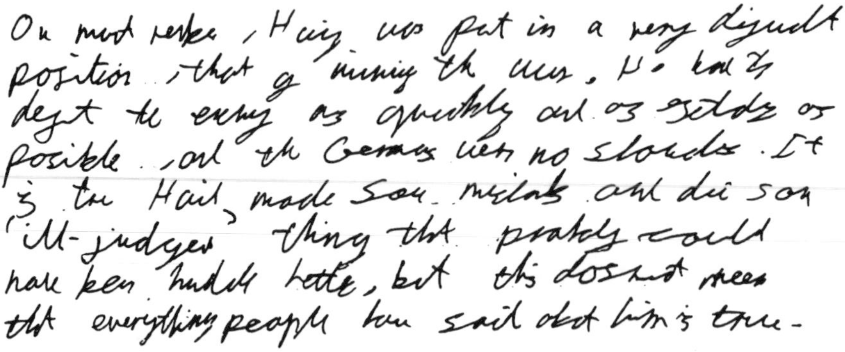

Under pressure of exams – in this case mock GCSEs – Tim's writing becomes even more illegible.

Example B

Question: Explain why there must be no air in a car's hydraulic brake system.

Answer:

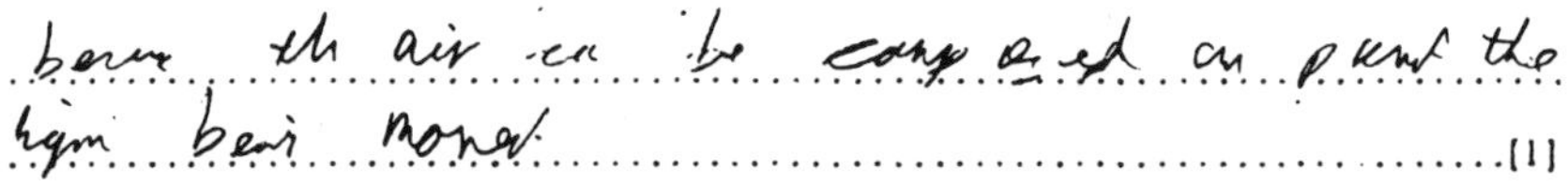

His school applied to the Examinations Board for a writer for the real GCSE exam in June, and this was granted.

However, it should be noted that, in the same way that the ability to recognise words when seen may lessen a reading problem, a strong kinaesthetic skill (that is, a feel for how the pen should move when writing) may overcome, or at least lessen, a spelling problem; hence the importance of joined-up writing (see Chapter 8, Handwriting). A comparison may be made with keyboard skills. At first the person is searching across the keyboard to find the required letter, but after practice the fingers pick up a pattern, and it is this pattern which takes over and becomes touch-typing. Interestingly, the operator usually has to search again for the individual letters when faced with postcodes, where no pattern prevails. An analogy may also be made with the automatic hand and foot movements when driving a car.

Typical mistakes

A teacher will be alerted to a dyslexic child's spelling problem by spelling that is either bizarre (for example, **wusf**/must) or purely phonic (such as **hipocrasy**/hypocrisy), and she should not be put off track if that child can, in fact, read quite well.

The following are typical mistakes made by dyslexic people, though it would be most unusual to find all of them made by one person:

1   The outline or shape of a word may be similar to the correct word, but some of the letters are confused:

e.g. **day**/dog   **tock**/took   **beteew**/between   **amiad**/animal

and **l**s may be crossed and **t**s left uncrossed, resulting in words like **onty**, **plenly**, **slitt**, and **Auslratia**.

2   The following letters may be reversed or mirrored:

$$\frac{b \mid d}{p \mid q\,g} \quad h/y \quad t/f \quad m/w \quad n/u \quad s/z$$

And these cause confusion as the reversal makes another letter. Other letters which are often reversed are:

ǝ ɔ ᵢ p ⅂ ᴚ ᒑ ᗡ Ↄ И

Spelling mistakes, such as these, may result:

de for be, **wusf** for must, **bog** or **bop** for dog, **unt** for nut, **bus** for bus, **ɔat** for cat, **jaw** for jam, **vomel** for vowel.

And also punctuation, such as:

3   The letters may be the correct ones but in the wrong order:

hlep for help, **felt** for left, **was** for saw, **on** for no, **hwo** or **how** for who, **being** for begin, **Jhon** for John, **hared** for heard.

4   The letters used may be those whose sounds are near to the correct ones:

> a/u/o, e/i, m/n, th/v/f, d/t, p/b, s/sh/ch, j/ch, g/k, n/ng

and this results in the following types of mistakes:

> **cat** for cut, **hup** for hop, **set** or **sid** for sit, **nat** for mat,
> **wip** for web, **sop** for shop.

5   The dyslexic person may be unaware of certain sounds, especially in blends:

> the **n** sound in **went**, with the result that he writes **wet**

and similar mistakes, such as **bup** or **bum** for bump, **pum** for plum, **cash** for crash, **trator** for tractor, **stars** for starts.

Conversely, when he has learnt letter-sound combinations like **nt**, **mp**, **pl** or **cr**, he may include them where it is unnecessary and for cap he writes **camp**, for pan he writes **plan**, etc.

6   Dyslexic children do not always realise that letters have names as well as sounds, and the following kinds of mistakes occur:

> **nd** for end, **flt** for felt, **tmper** for temper, **Pter** for Peter, **frm** for
> farm, **ms** for mess, **bgan** for began, **lft** for left, **tm** for team,
> **dp** for deep, **ct** for seat, **km** for came, **agn** for again.

7   Words or phrases may be foreshortened or telescoped:

> **rember** for remember, **sudly** for suddenly, **ner** for nearer, **horsn**
> for horizon, **spares** for sparkles, **cabin the wood** for cabin in the
> wood.

8   The dyslexic person may be confused over whether there should be one word or two words:

> **a bout, aslong as, yes terday, in stead.**

9   The hand does not always automatically do what the brain intends. A dyslexic person may be writing, for instance, king, but having started the curve of the **g** his hand takes the line up instead of down and instead of king he has unwittingly written **kind**.

Many of these mistakes are found in the writing of very young children, but normally disappear at 7–8 years. This does not happen in the case of dyslexic children, and these types of mistakes continue to be found in their written work.

Words tend to be spelt phonically, because children, when in doubt, often revert to phonic sounds and apply phonics to the best of their ability, as, for instance, **bubolls** for bubbles.

Here is a Hallowe'en poem written by Amy when she was 7 years 4 months. Amy is a very bright child and her grandfather is a poet; she appears to have inherited some of his talent. However, it can be seen that her dyslexic-type mistakes are not automatically disappearing.

Example C

Spiders' webs and frogs'
    legs,
Mix 'em up and stir 'em
    down.
Whiz, pop, fizz as the
    bubbles rise,
Add wriggling worms and
    pumpkin pies.
Add a bit of this and a bit
    of that,
Look at the eyes of the big
    black cat,
Twinkling as it sits on the
    mat.

She was beginning to feel frustrated and anxious about falling behind in class. When she was assessed by the educational psychologist, it was found that she had a Reading Accuracy Age of 6 years 5 months (Neale), Comprehension Age of 6 years 11 months (Neale) and a Spelling Age of 6 years 4 months (Vernon). With a Verbal IQ of 130, her reading and spelling should have been two to three years above her chronological age. With tuition from a dyslexia specialist, this gap began to close, and Amy was feeling happier and more confident. Later she was considering a course at university.

Some children are severely dyslexic, others moderately so, and many are merely mildly dyslexic, yet all dyslexic children will have some difficulties right from the start – difficulties with learning letters and which way round they face. They cannot visualise them, and if they have the letter in front of them they may be uncertain – even after being taught – how to form the letter (see Chapter 8, Handwriting). They may easily get letters back to front or upside down.

All children starting school will need time to sort these things out, but with the dyslexic child the uncertainty persists. He needs much more time spent on the basic learning skills before he becomes sure of the sound–symbol relationship of letters and how to write them. Even then there will be lapses. If teachers and parents do not understand, early on he will begin to feel under pressure. He sits there in class and others around him get their letters right, write words and are praised. The non-visualiser of words is unable to understand why it just does not happen for him. The teacher will need to find out how he visualises in his mind's eye (see Chapter 1, Dyslexia). If he is unable to create an accurate image of the word (that is, there is no word-picture), she knows that he has no visual basis for spelling. If when writing *cat* he starts mouthing c-a-t, he tends to rely on letter-sounds. For him, phonics is the way forward.

Example D

Mary, aged 7 years 6 months, has written **One day two small boys went camping**. Having changed schools several times, because of her father's work, it is easy to put the cause of her illiteracy down to these changes. However, she has no visual recall for words or understanding of sound–symbol relationships. She needs help along the lines of Guide 1 (see page 76).

Example E

Even a child's own name may still be a problem at nearly 11 years old, despite good average intelligence.

Example F

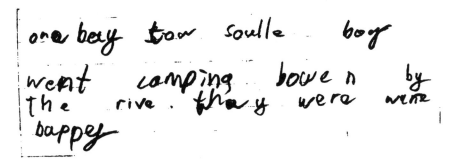

Here can be seen **b/d** confusion and **h/b** confusion; also uncertainty whether **happy** ends in **ey** or **y**. Written as a fusion, it is a useful ploy to hedge one's bets. Perhaps this child would benefit from a **bed** clue card beside him or **bed** pencilled at the top of the page (Fig. 4), whenever he writes. He could also learn that the left 'thumbs up' sign represents 'b' and the right 'd', as in Fig. 5. These points would be enough for the teacher to take up initially.

Fig. 4   Fig. 5

Sam, almost 12 years old, was invited to explain how the minute minder on the cooker was operated. He knew instinctively how to work it, but this is his written explanation (see Example G).

Example G

Example H

> In my nanny grden I walk as a lilte boy. As gone code weds drush aganst my pall pech fase when I go to the poll to skim the pedas. But to my astonsmnt as big as you colde amayn wlde us a calss romm I trow a ston ut it gave a roar I gumet out of the way it said Helw I golpt m I said He siad whily are you amast b b b b beauccase you cccc can talk that is not amazing yes it is. stap agving I will tell you abot my old home in the prohistoric land what I said yes He said I glpt agin sit dons alwrith I said nhaw tell my abot your old home yes He said when I was a lilte boy like you but a analm...

Emily, aged 9 years 7 months, has written the story in Example H above. Many of the points mentioned on pages 67–8 (points 1–9) are highlighted here, as well as lack of punctuation and structure of ideas.

Mistakes include confusing the name of the letter with its sound and transposing the order of letters, as well as doubling the wrong letter. Initially, she needs tuition in letter–sound associations and past tense *-ed* endings. Note the common error of 't' uncrossed and 'l' crossed in **lilte**.

Example I(i)

> The space code!
>
> "Calling caplen Buz"
> Buz run to the rocke "yes Buz
> speing"
> "the Big B wrtes you in the Bass BBp
> Buz said Buz to the terter

Example I(ii)

my werst lie

I was on my Holerday with my grannar. My siter and I alluase go to wails for 2 weeks in the summar Holerdays. My cuson (mikel) lived in the next villy me and my cuzon whonted to mack a bass so he came over and then we went over to the woods opsit. We made sume traps all a round the new bilt Bass then I desid I no to mack a Bow. mikel went off to find sum wood. I looked up at the trees then I looked back down at Kniff going up and down the bow then I sliped and the Kniff cut me in three different poses I was worred be coss I was not a lowed a Kniff it was to beep to put a plaster on it so I toled my grann I triped up over sum pucl wier.

Andrew wrote Example I(i) when he was 12 years 5 months. His Reading Accuracy at that time was 6 years and his Spelling Age 7 years 1 month. After a term and a half with specialist tuition in a school for dyslexic boys, the improvement in both spelling and handwriting can be seen in Example I(ii). He is using his knowledge of phonics enabling all words to be read and understood. Joined-up writing shows good kinaesthetic development, which in turn will help to improve his spelling.

'The Wizard's Cat' (Example J, page 74) by Robert, aged 9 years, shows a number of the typical mistakes mentioned in points 1–9 (pages 67–8). It would be tempting to correct too many different types of error in a piece of work like this. At least Robert has the confidence to set to and write an imaginative story and should be given credit for content. He has also managed **they** not **thay** seven out of eight times, which was a good step forward for him.

If the teacher wants Robert to read back what he has written, this will need to be done at the time of writing because later he, too, may be unable to translate it. In both **shret** (street) and **monsh** (monster) he has written **sh** instead of **st**. This could be a good starting point for the teacher. Work with a mirror would show him how the spoken sounds should link to the letters.

What would the reader suggest as the next step?

Example J

The wivds Cat

One barcl Rnigh wen they
was not a saund but a aul
in nomb One vils shret
a lit boy sen till a vere
store lat ball hade two glowing
ise the cart sunt ot say
come on lets have a flit
oft made lik land it sed
so thensed holld my
hand so they bapt them
selfs to a land fure a
waya in time but they land
idt at the grawd wot was
sand they was up sidawn then
a monsh no hed sepen then
so they run on throo booshis
and they swam thoo Jacks
spile the cat lict it they finer-
le got aut of sit os thay
came ot a wood so they sat

Example K

> Yes my Geomerty has deaftly improved
> rember I was always flooding into tears
> of my disastces results.
>   I am in the school chess
> team, and just brought a game of
> Risk which is very interging.
>   Yours Sincerly

Sadly, this boy eventually found the pressures of failure too great, and committed suicide.

Example L

4 | the Suorjc Je Drmd the Forb .

5 | a Corld Norf weind iS BLoring.

4 The soldier stormed the fort.
5 A cold north wind is blowing.

Bobby, 12 years 6 months, is bright but disruptive in class because of frustration. The two sentences in Example L were dictated. Bobby has not attained the National Curriculum targets. He has no literacy skills and before long will be starting the GCSE syllabus. Although he is now receiving some tuition from a dyslexia specialist, she is only able to see him for one hour a week in a small group. Although the gap between complete illiteracy and a spelling age required to meet his potential intellectual needs is just beginning to lessen, he will inevitably be faced with the GCSE syllabus without the necessary skills to tackle it.

Spelling conventions

Language is structured; each language has its own conventions. For instance, **silent E** lengthens vowels in English; in Dutch doubling vowels has a similar function. Early written language followed a sound–symbol basis as closely as possible, bearing in mind local dialects and the symbols of the alphabet available. Later, various conventions, such as the different uses of **C**, **K** and **CK** were devised by scribes and grammarians as spelling became more standardised.

English *appears* to be lacking in a logical approach, partly because pronunciation has changed over the centuries, but also because each invasion and settlement brought a new language – Anglo-Saxon, Old Norse/Danish and French – all with their own spelling conventions which have eventually become assimilated into English. Latin and Greek words were also incorporated into the language. Each of these languages has its own structure.

Later still, in 1755, Dr Johnson standardised spelling in his dictionary. However, even today there are alternative spellings; for example, **ageing/aging, recognise/recognize, gaol/jail, connection/connexion**.

Many children are fascinated by information on the history of their language and they then begin to appreciate the reasons for apparently illogical English spelling.

Spelling guides

As many children have to learn to read through learning to spell, they need a structured approach, and this approach should be multisensory. The following guidelines are for class teachers; they may select from these according to the needs of their pupils. Detailed programmes are available for specialists teaching children with severe problems. A simple way to introduce letters (see Guide 1 below) can be used by a class teacher to get a non-starter off the ground.

Guide 1

(Letter *sounds* are in lower case, letter *names* in upper case.)

Children learn early to recognise their first names and the sounds of the first letter of their names.

Suppose a child is called Pat.

Take the first letter **p** – say the **sound** – get the child to watch your lips and whisper **p-p-p**. (It is important to give the pure sound **p**, without schwa; that is, added vowel-sound as **per**.) Write **p** on a small piece of paper or, better still, a piece of card.

Put a line under the letter to indicate which way round it goes.

Then, perhaps, take the **m**-sound for **mum** and go through the same process – again, as with every letter, avoiding the added schwa.

Then **t** for, perhaps, **tomato, tiger** or his brother **Tom**. (Capital letters will need an explanation.)

Then, perhaps, **a** for **apple** or **alphabet**.

This should be written in red because it is a vowel.

Here, then, are four letters, which after discussion of sounds and shapes should be placed in front of the child. Now ask him to point to **m**, giving the letter *sound* (*not* name at this stage). If he gets it correct, he takes it. Proceed to another letter, whispering **p**, reminding him of his name. If he fails to get it correct, leave it for the moment and go on to, perhaps, **a** and then **t**. When he has linked all *sounds* correctly to each letter, place the letters back in front of the child, and this time point to each letter in turn asking the child to give the sound. After this little exercise the child has linked sound to shape and shape to sound of four letters, all of which have a particular meaning for him.

Now for the word-building! A phonically-regular word can be made up out of three of the letters.

pat, mat, tap, map

(Discuss the meanings of each word as it is given.)

Gradually other letters are included, for example, **n** for nasty, nice or a friend Nick.

nap, pan, man, tan,

and **e** for **egg**, giving **ten, men, pen, pet.**

These letters can be kept in an envelope or box. Many a small child, having battled with the Look-Say method and finding it incomprehensible, has begun to understand, by this simple technique, what reading and spelling are all about.

Names of letters should be gradually included. A capital letter for the child's name has to be mentioned at this stage, and can be related to the fact that the child is important and his name is special.

This links up easily with Jolly Phonics and other phonic-based schemes such as Letterland (Pictogram). Many infant and primary schools are familiar with Letterland (Pictogram), which provides memory tags for all the letters and digraphs; for instance, **W – wicked water witch.** This is very helpful for the child who cannot visualise a letter.

Reproduced by kind permission of Lynn Wendon (Letterland 1989)

Structured multisensory teaching programmes, such as Teaching Reading through Spelling (TRTS), based on the Hickey Multi-Sensory Language Course, use cards with letter or blend on one side and keyword picture on the other.

Phono-graphix, devised by Carmen and Geoffrey McGuiness in the US, is a reading and spelling programme that was originally for use on a 1:1 basis, but has subsequently been adapted for class tuition.

The Edith Norrie Letter-Case, which is a useful piece of remedial equipment, highlights the vowels in red, enabling pupils to see that there must be at least one vowel (that is, a splash of red) in every monosyllabic word, and, later, red in every syllable; it also helps to reinforce other spelling guides.

Use of proper terms, such as vowels and consonants, teaches children early on to be familiar with these terms. If a child has difficulty discriminating between short-vowel sounds he will need a lot of practice, especially between e and i. However, a short-vowel clue card (which he can make) is a useful device. The initial sound of each picture gives the accurate short-vowel sound – apple, egg, igloo, orange, umbrella. For American children the initial sound of octopus may be more accurate than orange.

This can be kept by him – possibly used as a bookmark – so that he can refer to it at any time.

Guide 2

The order of teaching spelling conventions will vary according to pupils' needs and the teacher's discretion. For the purpose of this book, some blends and digraphs have been grouped but should not necessarily all be taught together:

Consonant digraphs, such as:	**ch sh th wh**
Initial blends, such as:	**bl cl fl gl pl sl spl** **br cr dr fr gr pr tr** **str spr scr sw**
Final blends, such as:	**nt st ng mp nd nk**

have to be learnt and practised.

A mirror is included with the Edith Norrie Letter-Case so that the pupil can see – and then become aware of – what is happening in the mouth. Blends do not then need to be taught separately. In fact, it is always worthwhile for a teacher to provide a mirror for the child to observe his mouth while forming these consonant sounds and blends or, if no mirror is readily available, to observe the teacher's mouth. This can be done by a class teacher just as well as a special needs teacher.

Guide 3

Silent E represents a big step in both reading and spelling. If the vowels are in red it highlights how a final E lengthens the previous vowel. This provides a visual memory tag to reinforce the difference in sound:

e.g.	hat	–	hate	pet	–	Pete	bit	–	bite
	man	–	mane				fin	–	fine
	rat	–	rate						
	cap	–	cape	hop	–	hope	tub	–	tube
	gap	–	gape	not	–	note	us	–	use

Guide 4

The murmuring vowels

ar or er ir ur

and common simple vowel digraphs

-ai -ay, -ee -ea, -oi -oy, -ou -ow

but murmuring vowels and digraphs with the same sounds, such as **er/ir/ur/** and **ee/ea** should be taught separately – possibly with a gap of a week or two between them – to avoid confusion.

Guide 5

After a short vowel, double the consonant before the following vowel (unless there are already two consonants, as in ca**mp**er):

e.g. planner, scatter, better, swimming, shopping, muddy.

As a spelling guide is taught children all too readily pick on exceptions. For this reason the term **guide** has been used rather than **rule**.

Latin-derived words cut across many spelling guides because the conventions in that language were different:

e.g. **animal, family** do not have a double consonant after the short vowel-sound.

Most words in a young child's vocabulary follow spelling guide 5. Latin-derived words are often more sophisticated and are therefore used by older children.

Guide 6

-**ed** endings:

e.g. jump**ed**, bang**ed**, walk**ed**, crook**ed**

-**le** words:

Compare short-vowel as in b**attle**, k**ettle**, p**uddle**
long-vowel as in t**able**, t**itle**, n**oble**

A line is drawn down the centre of a page in an exercise book with headings 'short-vowel' and 'long-vowel' on each side. The teacher then gives a variety of these -**le** words so that each child has to think of the word structure and write them in the appropriate column.

Guide 7

Spelling guidelines such as the need for **dge**, **tch** and **ck** which follow a single short vowel; also the appropriate use of **C** and **K**.

Guide 8

Plurals – words ending in **Y**. If the **Y** is preceded by a consonant, change **Y** to **I** and add **ES**:

e.g. baby – bab**ies**
strategy – strateg**ies**

If a vowel precedes **Y**, only add **S**:

monkey – monkey**s**
tray – tray**s**

Guide 9

Syllables

Children should be taught that there must be one **vowel-sound** in each syllable (beat of a word):

> e.g.   one beat – **boy, cake**
>
> two beats – **birth-day, class-room, car-pet**
>
> three beats – **un-der-stand**

Tapping out the number of syllables and being sure that at least one vowel occurs in each prevents foreshortening words:

> e.g.   **rember** (remember), **sudly** (suddenly)

Y acts as a vowel in words such as carry and my.

If a child has no feeling for rhythm, get him to hold a pencil and the teacher hold his hand – in this way he experiences the rhythm via the teacher (see Chapter 3, Speech and language processing). A comparison may be made with the African talking drums. Many messages have been sent throughout Africa by beating out the rhythm of the words on drums. In times gone by, explorers were often surprised to find that their arrival in a village was expected; the drums had already conveyed the information.

Syllable division

In saying the words aloud in their separate syllables, older children will develop an awareness of closed and open syllables.

Diacritical marks (distinguishing marks) for short- and long-vowels can be explained, and children then understand how they are used in dictionaries as an aid to pronunciation of unknown words:

> e.g.   closed   open
>
> **bŭn**   **tūlip**

The long vowel at the end of an open syllable is spelt with the vowel by itself, not a digraph:

bā con

e.g. not **baicon** or **baycon**

Guide 10

Information on the structure of words should include prefixes and suffixes and their meanings. This gives children insight into the meanings of whole words too, and the grammatical links of certain spelling families:

e.g. stem (root) – struct (from Latin, build)

		struct	ure	
		struct	ur al	
		struct	ur al	ly
	in	struct		
	in	struct	ive	
	in	struct	ion	
	re	struct	ure	
	con	struct	ive	
	con	struct	ing	
re	con	struct	ing	
	con	struct	ion	
	de	struct	ion	
	ob	struct	ive	
	ob	struct	ion	
	super	struct	ure	
	infra	struct	ure	

Prefixes

in	=	in
re	=	again
con	=	together
de	=	away from
ob	=	in the way of
super	=	over
infra	=	below

Suffixes

ive	=	indicating action, towards action
ion	=	result of action, condition

ure	=	process, function
ing	=	continuous action
ly	=	like, in such a manner

There are a number of structured spelling programmes on the market, and selected information at a teacher's discretion is interesting for a whole class. It is advocated in the National Curriculum that children should be aware of the structure of the language.

All this information on language structure should be peppered with mnemonics and illustrations to help children remember tricky spellings; for example, There is **a rat** in se**para**te; ne**c**essary 1 collar, 2 socks; my **pal** is the princi**pal** of the college; I a**cc**ept a change; she h**ears** with her **ears**; a se**cret**ary keeps her boss's **secret**.

A new memory tag could be written on a corner of the board at the beginning of each week.

Some dyslexic children have no understanding of punctuation, nor feeling for what comprises a sentence. Capital letters, commas and full stops are scattered around, but seldom in the correct places. It has to be carefully explained that a sentence is a group of words that makes sense, and that expressions such as **in the garden** and **as they went for a walk** leave one with the feeling that more information is needed about what is happening. Therefore, they are not complete sentences. Teachers need to work on sentence structure so that what is written is clear.

The following example was written by a very intelligent 17-year-old boy.

Example M

I was thinking that if there is a spool tape recorder at the center (like the one you had). I saw one there when I was last up there . . . . The reason why I think that some took head phones may help. Last night I listened to a tape and I found my mind was not completely concentrating and with head phones it may make a differences.

Difficulties in acquiring correct spelling

It cannot be emphasised too strongly that children are seldom able to remember a spelling guide the first time it is given. Dyslexic children will need considerable reinforcement – with *no criticism* of their forgetfulness, because rectifying spelling is a very difficult process for dyslexic people.

Workbooks are useful for reinforcing spelling guides, but correct exercises in a workbook are not necessarily an indication that a spelling pattern has been mastered. Mistakes on that pattern may well occur in general written work. The child may have been able to see the logic and pattern within a set exercise, but may not have absorbed it so that he can use it in another context. This, of course, applies to all children, but the dyslexic child needs *more time* before the information is used automatically. If clues in a textbook or their own folder are not available to dyslexic children, the real situation soon becomes apparent in any piece of free writing where they have to concentrate on content more than on spelling and handwriting.

Another area of illusion may be the weekly spelling tests. Many a dyslexic child can learn the ten or twenty words sufficiently well the night before to get by in the test the following day. The class teacher then has *proof* with marks such as 15/20 or even 20/20 that the child is *all right*, and she may use these test results to reassure an anxious parent, possibly pointing out that poor spelling in his free writing is just carelessness. However, if any of the words in the spelling test are included in the following week's test, it is usually found that they have, by then, been forgotten (see Example N, page 86). Correct spellings were given on the board at the end of this test and each boy marked his own, sometimes correcting as he went. Consequently, some words are marked wrong when appearing correct.

Some parents may need to be alerted to the fact that learning spellings for the weekly spelling test may need their help, otherwise it will be altogether too demanding. Some guidance for parents along the lines mentioned will probably be appreciated.

The fact that correct spelling has not become automatic and therefore needs to be given so much attention may result in *either*:

> I   Diverting the writer from the subject-matter because his work is geared to words that he feels confident in spelling and therefore he loses the thread; more often, though, it gives rise to immature vocabulary and expression in order to be confident of the spelling.

Example N

Spelling Test

1. Shoulders ✓
2. Rouge ✗
3. Tomorrow ✓
4. Toangue ✗
5. Sympthatec ✗
6. Surprize ✓
7. Tecbnical ✗
8. vegetable ✓
9. Yacht ✗   Yacht
10. Stationary ✓
11. Speech ✗
12. vallies Vallies ✗
13. Yoke ✗
14. Soaring Soaring ✗
15. Ridiculus ✗
16. Rhythma ✗
17. Saze ✗
18. santance ✗
19. sepperate ✗
20. Skillfull ✗
21. Solle ✗

Example O

On sunday ted the Bear went to
the stadle to find about His this
horse he went to his trap then
he went over to alkort he took
alkoft over to the trop he tele the
onto aldoot tet ted took ham ham
hum for askin

The story in Example O was written by Kit when he was aged 9 years 3 months. Kit is highly intelligent but continued, a year later, to have great problems with punctuation and sentence structure.

Or:

---

2   The child gets involved in what he wants to say, using a wider vocabulary and concentrating on his subject, and spelling then deteriorates. He may then be accused of carelessness because, when errors are pointed out, he can rectify them.

Example P

not answer any questions. To day there is
to be a court in ~~quirty~~. The magistrate
is Mr Hiatt. If anyone has seen a ~~b~~piglet
named Wallace who was missing after the
incident also missing are twelve Rhode Island
red ~~chickings~~ and an Aylesbury duck. If
anybody knows anything about the animals please
contact Mr Etchells of Much Bickering farm.

This is horribly tedious.

Likewise, if information is dictated in class by a subject teacher, it is extremely difficult to write what has just been dictated while taking in the information for the next sentence to be written (see Chapter 12, Study skills).

The old-fashioned way of getting a pupil to write out spelling corrections several times is often less than profitable and usually includes new misspellings as he progresses down the page (see Example Q). This may leave the teacher feeling apoplectic with anger and frustration while the pupil is sublimely ignorant of anything being amiss!

Example Q

immediately × 5

immediately
immediatley
immedatley
immedatley
immedatly

What teachers should not do

Justin was unable to find any structure or spelling patterns in his teacher's corrections and – perhaps fortunately for his morale – was unable to decode her comments. No encouragement was given for his good, imaginative story (see Example R, page 89).

If a child is then asked to re-write a corrected version of his work, which is often the case, it is virtually impossible for him to make use of his teacher's corrections and produce a good copy. It becomes even more difficult for him if he has to turn back a page while he is copying.

What teachers can do

Teachers should bear in mind that if the visual recall of a word is poor (like a photograph taken with a cheap, old camera) or non-existent (like a blank negative), then the pupil is thrown back on to auditory discrimination (phonics and word-building) and joined-up writing to develop the kinaesthetic or feel of the word.

Example R

I am a ~~toders~~ and .j.   P
swoop ~~llouber~~ rubber and ~~riiver~~ rniver ~~rist~~ rist. I kill ~~loentlls~~ turtles
and ~~shush~~ fish and some of the fish
hae ~~spies~~ spikes on ~~thes~~ their bock.
in the ~~junall~~ jungle there are big
hairy ~~Spider~~ and ~~the cach~~ they catch small
~~bentos~~ birds and eat them all up.
~~peecos~~ Peko's ~~sover~~ father bind big ~~hites~~
Msisx. peko ~~keke~~ Peko his ~~jaguer~~ saguar teeth.

Too many spelling mistakes and the
writing is untidy   (9)

> The skills needed for accurate spelling are:
>
> **1**   good visual recall of words, i.e. an accurate mental image;
>
> **2**   good auditory discrimination, i.e. an accurate awareness of letter-sounds, syllable-sounds and word-sounds;
>
> **3**   good kinaesthetic skill, i.e. feel for the patterning of the word through the movement of the hand while writing, *or*, the finger-patterning on a keyboard which produces correct spelling.

Improving visual recall

Methods advocated when using the Edith Norrie Letter-Case and NLP (Neuro-Linguistic Programming) use the strategy of looking carefully at a word, covering it, and trying to form a mental picture of it – then of being asked by the teacher such questions as:

1   How many letters are in the word?
2   Is there a vowel, or more than one vowel – or if vowels are in red, is there a red letter?
3   Are there more letters before or after the vowel/red letter?
4   Are there any tall/ascending letters?
5   Are there any descending letters?
6   What are the letters in the word? (Do not say **spell the word** because of unhappy connotations.)
7   Can you give me the letters of the word backwards, i.e. from right to left?
8   Can you now write the word in joined-up writing? This will then indicate whether the child has a secure knowledge of the spelling – but reinforcement will still be needed from time to time.

It may be necessary for the teacher to start with familiar objects rather than words – such as a child's bicycle (how many wheels, the colour?) and then, for instance, go on to ask about his bedroom (can he visualise it? the colour of the walls, where is the bed, what are the patterns on the curtains?) – leading on to a familiar word such as his name. Can he then see any words within his name?

e.g.   Richard   James

Rich / hard   Jam / am / me

Next come words of especial interest to the child. *This technique is particularly helpful for learning to spell irregular words.*

The above technique in no way replaces the need for phonics. A knowledge of phonics and the structure of words (spelling guides) is the key. It enables the pupil to decode words (that is, read) and encode (namely, spell).

Improving phonological awareness (auditory recall)

Many of the suggestions in Chapter 3, on Speech and language processing, are valid for improving spelling:

I	tapping or clapping syllables;
2	rhyming games;
3	making word families, e.g. **cat, mat, hat**
	injection, inspection, correction;
4	accurate repetition of polysyllabic words, and later of sentences.

Developing kinaesthetic techniques

The kinaesthetic techniques and SOS (Simultaneous Oral Spelling), whereby a child says the letters as he writes them, strengthens the memory for letters and the kinaesthetic flow. So indeed does the Fernald technique, and Charles Cripps' and Margaret Peters' Look-Cover-Say-Write-Check. Of the three channels – visual, auditory, kinaesthetic – it is a question of building on the strongest mode and training the weaker ones. It is for this reason that a multisensory technique is advocated, automatically covering all three.

General recommendations

Words for class spelling tests are often topic-based rather than grouped for structure, and the dyslexic child is totally at sea with words such as those shown in Example S.

Example S

kitchen	*kitchen*
cooker	*cokker*
electricity	*elexrisurty*
fridge	*frige*
freezer	*frezzer*
mixer	*mixer*
oven	*oven*
microwave	*mircovave*
saucepan	*saeepan*
breadboard	*bread bord*

He needs word families so that he can see how the structure works.

Example T

batch	*batch*
catch	*catch*
thatch	*fatch*
stretch	*stretch*
kitchen	*Kitchen*
hotch-potch	*hotch potch*
Dutch	*Dutch*
crutches	*chuteoruck crutches*
clutching	*clutching*
matches	*matches*

All spellings here are correct except where the child has written **fatch** for thatch, confusing **f** and **th**. *Meanings of words* should always be checked.

If there are one or two dyslexic children in the class, a short list of structure-based words for their weekly spelling will be far more helpful than random words, if this can be woven into the day's activities.

One spelling test can never be appropriate for a whole class. Some children may not even need to look at the words again before the test. Others work at them and can learn, but there will always be the few for whom it is a soul-destroying and daunting task; even if they were to spend all day on the list, they would still be making errors. Paired testing in which two mildly dyslexic children test each other on a few words may be more appropriate.

Young children and wordbooks

The teacher is faced with the choice of whether it is better to write the word correctly herself, perhaps using colour to highlight a difficult area, or to dictate the word letter by letter, or sound it out phonically for the child to write down. If at all possible, different children in the class should be given the word in the way most suited to their needs rather than having a general class rule.

Teenagers

For the teenage pupil taking examinations, spellings for subjects need particular attention. One useful way is to write 6–8 key words on a card which is then inserted at the back of the exercise book or folder. These are then readily available for reference, and as they are used often, the student will begin to become familiar with their correct spelling. As each one becomes automatic, it can be crossed out and another one added, according to the need for its use.

No matter how great the spelling problem, it is often better *initially* for thoughts to be written down uninhibited by concern for correct spelling. A pocket dictating machine may be useful so that ideas are first recorded and later transferred to paper, when more consideration may be given to both spelling and grammar which, of course, includes punctuation. Laptops are increasingly used in class.

A useful ploy when a student has written an essay is to select certain misspellings according to a particular spelling guide, for example, -ing words, and then get someone – perhaps a parent or good friend – to dictate back the essay. This time the student can give maximum consideration to improving spellings of words which he likes to use to express *his* thoughts. This has a direct influence on improving his own written work. This, of course, is where word-processors can be a great support.

When to call in outside professional help

> 1   A child of, for instance, 10 years with an average IQ should have a spelling age of about 10 years for his written work to be adequate for his intellectual needs.
>
> A child of 10 years with an IQ of about 120, or generally accepted to be bright, should have a spelling age of approximately 12 years to meet his intellectual needs.
>
> A child of, say, 10 years with an IQ of 90 should have a spelling age of approximately 9 years to cope adequately.

If a child is orally bright, but his spelling is poor, then a Wechsler Intelligence Scale for Children IQ test or British Ability Scales IQ test by a chartered educational psychologist will highlight where his learning difficulties lie.

But, remember that his IQ scores may well have been depressed by a speech and language-processing problem; and some sub-test scores are often depressed by a dyslexia problem, reducing the overall IQ (see Chapter 2, Ears, eyes and IQs, and Chapter 3, Speech and language processing).

NB: *Poor spelling is not an indication of low intelligence! Neither is good spelling necessarily an indication of high intelligence.*

> 2   Spelling ages on spelling tests may vary from one test to another, and, indeed, so does a person's performance. But if a class teacher is continually confronted by bizarre and indecipherable spellings or a child's individual use of phonics, a dyslexia specialist should be sought at the earliest opportunity in order to guide and help the class teacher and the pupil.

Mild to moderate dyslexic problems

A special mention needs to be made of children with mild to moderate dyslexic problems, for they often receive no specialist tuition and are put under constant pressure. They, too, need recognition and guidance in order to perform at the appropriate level, especially if they are obviously bright. They invariably feel inadequate in comparison with their peers. They also feel frustrated because they are unable to express themselves on paper at a level commensurate with their intellectual development. They seldom get credit, however much effort they put in. These children, too, would benefit from a multisensory structured approach to spelling. In fact, what is good for the dyslexic child is good for the non-dyslexic child too.

Chapter 8

Handwriting

Centuries ago, spoken words were the only means by which ideas could be conveyed. Then man found there were occasions on which he wished to leave messages for someone else, and he would do this by drawing pictures. Each sketch would depict a story or event. Gradually this means of communication was developed until one little picture, or pictograph, stood for a word. In turn, these pictographs were developed into more symbolic shapes known as 'ideographs'.

However, writing in this way was very slow and there were thousands of different ideographs to be learnt (as in Chinese) and so scholars hit upon the idea of using symbols for the limited number of sounds that went into spoken words, giving the foundations to the alphabets we know today. Phonetic spelling followed the period of pictographs and ideographs. Symbols were used for sound; one can still imagine a snake for the symbol S representing the hissing sound. These symbols have since become greatly simplified and now, in English, we need only twenty-six of them to express any idea under the sun.

Perhaps technological advances will eventually dispense with the need for written communication, but until such time, it is essential for people to be able to decode and encode these symbols.

Encoding, or writing, is a subject on which most teachers feel qualified to comment, and the way in which the letters should be written invariably produces a wealth of argument and opinions. Some teachers feel that children print to avoid confusion when reading, but reading and writing are not the same activity and it is a fallacy to believe that it is essential for a child to read *and* write the exact same shape to avoid confusion.

Every primary school in the UK has to have a handwriting policy, so does every State in Australia. The National Curriculum requires that handwriting should be specifically taught, as it used to be, so that children know where to begin and how to form the letters. Fashions and teachers change and various types of writing have emerged. Italic, cursive, printed, looped, plain or script – all have their disciples ready to pass on the *right* way, the exclusive use of which, it is often claimed, would ensure that everybody has beautiful handwriting.

It is all too easy to forget how very complex the act of writing is, particularly for people who may never have encountered personal difficulty in this area. By using the analogy of a foreign language the frustrations of a non-reader and poor speller may be readily understood, but there seems to be no comparable analogy to arouse the sympathy of a teacher who is faced with chaos in the actual formation of letters and words. Therefore, it is important to stop and consider some of the reasons behind the scrawl which is so often a feature of the dyslexic person's work.

Reasons for poor handwriting at any age

Poor motor control

For neurological reasons, some students may find extreme difficulty in manipulating and guiding the pen. They know the shape the letters should be, but, try as they may, they are unable to reproduce controlled curves and angles. This difficulty in manipulation may only manifest itself in fine control or it may be a more extensive problem (see Example A).

Example A

Malformed letters

The pupil who has directional confusion in the formation of a letter, or who hesitates over the actual shape, is all too often unable to begin, continue and complete a letter in the conventional manner – see Examples B (i) and (ii). Furthermore, there are those who are unable to picture the shapes of certain letters they wish to produce (see Example C). Others have been writing in a certain way for so long that the wrong groove is already set.

Example B

(i)

(ii)

Example C

Tension

Fear of failure to write legibly or spell correctly, fear of a teacher's anger or ridicule of his work – all may result in a general lack of self-confidence and give rise to a very tense child. Consequently, he grips the pen tightly, restricting all natural fluency of movement and overworking several muscles unnecessarily. Tension can settle at the back of the neck, causing the child to need to twist the head and shrug the shoulders in order to try to relieve it. The hand and arm tire quickly and may ache, giving rise to further tension. The end result is the all too usual, cramped and jagged writing – see Examples D (i) and (ii). Swinging on monkey bars at break or in the park, helps to relieve this tension.

Example D

(i)

> At the age of ten years he Started working in the mill helping to make cloth for to meny a drapper in his own cowntrey and in England and W ales. He worked till 8 o'clock in the evening and then went to knight School. There was no eseape from hard work if he wanted to be a dockter.

(ii)

> When they got of The boat they drove south until they case to a brige. They stopd beause they did not know if they soud go to the left or the right. There was a man sitting beside the road and they asked him the way.

Speed

Children are always in a hurry to finish, either before writing is wiped from the board or when there are other activities they are wanting to do. They also have difficulty copying accurately, which leaves little or no time for concentrating on the look of the end product. Even when not copying, extra time is needed to try to work out spelling. Homework often takes two or three times longer than it should and the messy result may leave the teacher with the impression that little time or effort has been spent (see Example E, page 100).

Example E

① in the evening, the fishermen dragged in their nets hopping to find a large catch of fish in them.

② Mrs ~~After~~ Adams drove to the market for some pork chops I cant afford them she grumbled to her self as she saw the prices that where marked on the tags.

③ The Speakers introduction was so long that it put every one to sleep. However this did not seem to deter him And he groaned on and on.

Size

Small, cramped writing is often produced in order to disguise weak spelling (see Example F).

Example F

. They   became   to grow tired of throwing snow

balls   and became   to make   a snow man. But the wind

became   to blow   and the soft snow slowly become

hard. Lights glowed in the   windows and they followed

the grown-ups   home hopping that the snow would be back

again   tomorow.

It may also be the large spiky uncontrolled type (see Example G).

Example G

Those who enjoy football will know that rugby rules permit a player to run while holding the ball.

The game of rugby began in 1823 when a boy at rugby school picky up the football and ran with it in his arms.

Hesitations

Fluency is lost as the pen stops and starts midway through sentences, words and even letters, while the pupil works out how to express ideas, spell the words or form the letters – see Example H (i) and (ii).

Example H

(i) *We gave the driver the signell. He put his foot down and rased off sending the man FLYING. He took his stick and looked at us. As he looked to where the bus look off to he started to run towards the vast land. We ran after him. He got tangeld in some barbed wire. He got louse Jimmy jumped up at him but he hit him over the head and he fell to the ground yelling. He run on. He seped and hit the ground and whiler he run on again. Fred jampd urat him and got hit.*

(ii) *Unles you shift i will be sick on your masters boat he said. Ag Aorg Agwotes Agus Augustus felt a tug and just intime his head was ses suspended over the ege of the boat*

Alterations

For messy crossings out or one letter superimposed on another in the hope that the correct version will be read (see Example I).

Example I

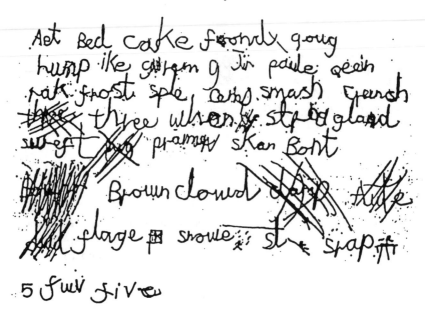

Earlier teaching

Although a child may have been shown correct letter formation, he may have slipped into bad habits which have not been corrected because the writing has been reasonably neat. This can give rise to problems later when he is learning to join letters. Left-handed children are often at a greater disadvantage, and are further handicapped by the fact that the hand they are writing with immediately covers what they have just written. If a pen is being used, the ink is smudged. Some right-handed teachers find it difficult to help left-handers with correct position and pencil grip (see page 106).

Suggestions for dealing with the problem

'You must improve your writing' is a remark that has been made to countless schoolchildren, and exercises of copying and re-writing are often handed out indiscriminately. These do little to touch the roots of the difficulty.

The first step is discussion in general terms of the advantages of good writing and the goals to be achieved. These goals are that the pupil should write easily, comfortably, fluently and legibly. This is far more important than having a particular style or scheme that is to be followed at all costs. The dyslexic person has so much to contend with that there is no point in insisting on change for its own sake.

The advantages of improvement may need to be spelt out in simple terms, as there may be little motivation on the part of pupils who are thoroughly disenchanted with the subject after constant nagging. These are:

- increase of speed;
- end of writer's cramp;
- approval to be gained;
- better marks in examinations, and the end of marks deducted for untidiness;
- the need to be able to read what has been written – the child will not act upon a teacher's comments at the end of his work if he has not been able to read it;
- confidence when faced with writing personal letters.

Older pupils may feel that it is childish to revert to basic exercises and letter-formation, but analysis of common faults in writing is the basis of improvements. It is useful to have samples, or a teacher may write a few well-chosen words on the board for comment, each showing a single fault and each exaggerated. Use the same words in each and read them out so that the pupil is concentrating on the writing rather than the content. Make sure that the pupils point out the fault themselves, which they are usually more than happy to do, especially when the writing is the teacher's! The following points may usefully be illustrated as they are often to be found at any age:

1 Writing that is too small

The car was slipping and sliding as they drove down the muddy track.

2 Writing that is too big

The car was

3 Uneven size of lower-case letters

The Car was Slipping and sliding

4 Upper-case letters, ascenders and descenders out of proportion

The car was slipping and suding as they

5 Inadequate or uneven spacing between letters

The car was slipping a nd sliding as they

6 Inadequate or uneven spacing between words

The   carwas .   slippingandsliding

7 Erratic slant

The cor was slipping and sliding

8 Malformed letters

The car was slipping cnd

9 Alterations

The car ~~was~~ was ~~slip~~ slipping

10 Inability to keep on line

The car was slipping and sliding

11 Specific letter problem appropriate to pupil

The car was slipping

12 No fault

The car was slipping and sliding as they

Encourage the pupils to study their writing and to decide for themselves where faults lie and what improvements can be made. It is often helpful to emphasise the fact that there are several faults which they do *not* make!

The importance of pupils deciding for themselves where steps should be taken for improvement cannot be overstressed. They are being self-critical and no resentment is built up at yet another person complaining about their work. This, of course, does not apply if teaching infants or young children, when the sound, shape, look and feel of letters are taught with a multisensory approach. As handwriting is, once again, being taught as a class subject, what has been suggested is equally appropriate for groups or individuals.

Some teachers think that children are confused by different formation of letters being used in reading and writing. In practice, the authors must say that they never have found this to be a problem.

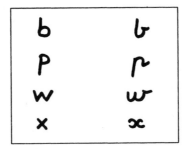

To show the child that they are in fact the same letters, the following idea may be helpful. This particular example links to Letterland (Pictogram). Write the printed form of the letter on a card and superimpose a sheet of tracing paper on which is the cursive letter. The cursive letter is then seen exactly over the printed form.

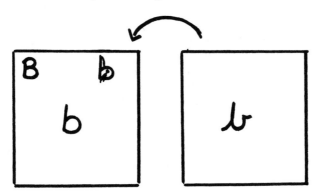

In order to achieve the best writing it is important to be in the most comfortable position with the correct height of desk and chair.

The pencil should be supported lightly and not gripped tightly. Show the pupil how it should be possible to whisk the pencil or pen away from his fingers without lifting his hand too, and that white knuckles are an indication of a tense grip.

The paper should be angled comfortably according to the handedness of the writer and anchored with the non-writing hand.

The portion of the forearm just in front of the elbow should rest on the edge of the table to form a pivot. If done correctly this position will allow a free swing to be made across the paper while keeping the wrist straight. This ensures that the table does the hard work of supporting the arm and hand, which therefore tire far less quickly.

It is important to maintain the pivot, and to do this the anchor hand should be used to move the page upwards from the writer as he progresses down the page.

Usually, this will result in a right-handed person writing with a slight slant forwards and a left-handed person with a slight slant backwards. Either is equally permissible unless carried to extremes. Fortunately, most people have ceased to look upon the natural back slant of a left-handed writer as a sign of a weak character!

Traditional sloping desks encouraged a good posture for writing. Modern adjustable equivalents are available, but even a large firm book, board or folder may be propped at an angle sloping towards the child. This will provide a comfortable position so that the shoulders do not hunch and the head does not drop forward.

For any physical activity, even if sedentary, there is a proper or best position while the body is balanced for that particular action. For instance, one has to be properly balanced for riding a bicycle, hitting a cricket ball, riding a pony, **and writing**. Looking round a class, children can soon see who looks right.

Point out that there are six simple shapes which go to make up all our letters.

Be prepared for the pupil with poor motor-control to have difficulty with these despite their simplicity. Such a pupil will benefit from colouring and completing dot-to-dot pictures, tracing over letters with the finger and doing exercises to practise pencil control (see below), before attempting writing.

Then attempt these shapes in these three units, the larger the better initially.

A board is useful for this, as is writing in the air, progressing on to sheets of newspaper. It is well to remember that some children experience problems in changing from the vertical to the horizontal plane. A really large, thick felt pen or wax crayon which offers little resistance to the paper may be useful for those with poor motor-control or those who have difficulty in holding a pencil correctly. It can be helpful to thicken the pencil with Blu-Tack or plasticine, which can then be moulded to the shape most easily managed by the individual pupil. Triangular pencils and pencil grips, which are easily obtainable, are useful for some children.

As control of the letter-shape improves, decrease the size and graduate to soft, then harder pencils and finally to a pen. Ball-point pens are not to be recommended as most writing appears to deteriorate with them. Modern instant-drying fibre-tipped pens are a boon, particularly to the left-handed (because their writing is not smudged as the hand moves over), and have the advantage that the finished product looks as if a conventional ink has been used.

Not only should the pupil have control when he is looking, but he should practise with his eyes shut so that he is not always dependent on his visual sense. In this way he is developing the kinaesthetic sense, in the same way that a competent knitter can also watch television. This will stand him in good stead when he can give full concentration to the content and spelling of his work rather than to the formation of his writing.

Once the size is down to exercise-book level, it is better to use lined paper to provide a stable base-line from which to work. Some people with poor spatial sense benefit from double-lined paper, and some may even need to use squared paper in order to produce uncramped letters. However, prolonged use of these can inhibit the natural fluency one is trying to develop, if the writer is labouring to fit the letters exactly between the lines. For initial practice the same can be achieved on a larger scale by the columns of the financial index pages of a newspaper being turned sideways to give well-spaced lines.

More children with poor handwriting appear to gain speed and fluency, and indeed to make fewer spelling mistakes, if they are encouraged to join their writing rather than to print it. However, there is always the exception, and the teacher must be flexible on this point if necessary. Fortunately, more class teachers are recognising that there is not a set age or class at which joined writing should be introduced. The earlier the links are taught and practised, the better the fluency and speed of writing and spelling (see Chapter 7, Spelling).

Joined writing does much for the confidence of the child. Every time the pen is lifted from the paper there is a greater chance of error when it is replaced. Cursive writing helps to eliminate the tendency of some pupils to insert upper-case letters in the middle of a sentence.

In practising, a child may need initially to trace over exercises done on card by the teacher, but this should be done for the minimum amount of time, as the pupil needs to develop his own rhythms. It is possible to coax a child into repeating an exercise several times without his feeling there is a set number of lines to be done. Ask him to do two lines, then to colour over the better sample, and then to try to do just one more. Then, perhaps, challenge him to better his best so far.

No word fills an entire line, and to build up a natural rhythm exercises are more useful if done in units of three. Complete lines are useless, because words are not written that way and the flow is lost. Anybody writing a complete, joined line of a single letter will find that the formation deteriorates towards the end.

Letter formation

In cursive script each letter ends with a tail, giving the links for joined writing, but for a child with severe directional difficulties the lead-in from the line gives him a reference point. He may need a small chart to serve as a constant reminder.

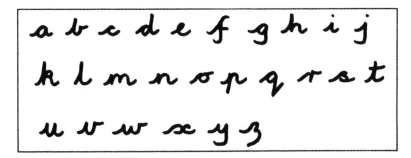

Loops at the top of letters tend to make writing untidy; but in order to keep the flow of cursive writing it seems reasonable to make loops on *g* , *j* , *y* and *ʒ* as a direct link back to the base-line. If the loop is taught as a direct joining line as opposed to a loop, there is less likelihood of extremes, for example, *g* not *ℬ* . Furthermore, many prefer printed **k** , **x** and **z** , which are quite acceptable but not so easily joined.

It has been suggested that the open *b* and *p* are less readily reversed than **b** and **p** , but there is little point in changing the style for these alone. Legibility and fluency are the goals rather than one particular style.

A well-rounded letter *c* is a good starting point for improving handwriting. Having achieved this, it can then be joined in a unit of three *ccc* . This leads naturally on to *a*, then *d*, *g* and finally, with a slight change, to *e* .

Practise these units, or short words made up of this group of **cadge** letters and, although other letters are being used in general work, it is usually helpful if only these letters are used in any writing practice until satisfactory results are obtained.

The next group includes those that determine the slant of the writing. This can be emphasised by taking a pencil or crayon and elongating the strokes, aiming to keep them roughly parallel.

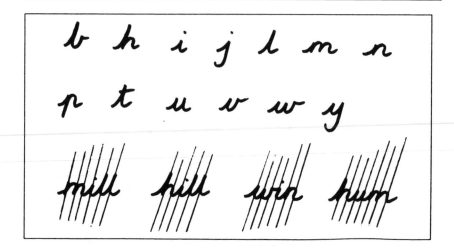

The third group is a combination of curves and angles.

If the angular printed **k** and **x** and **z** are used they introduce quite new directional strokes which detract from the overall effect, but many teachers and general writing schemes prefer this form.

Finally, the problem group which can be formed in more than one way and consequently can be confusing.

If **f** is used, the lower loop can be made either to the left or to the right; badly formed letters can be improved simply by suggesting that the pupil changes to the alternative side.

Upper-case letters are all begun at the top of the letter and on the left if there are two or more down strokes.

Reinforcement both of letter-formation and sequencing of the alphabet is given by writing the alphabet out three times, in units of three letters. Each letter has then been practised as it would occur initially, centrally or terminally in a word,

abc def ghi .... *yza* ....

ending on the third time round with

xyz

If practice is needed in writing, it is essential to use words which present no problem to the child in terms of meaning or spelling.

If a passage is used as writing practice, fluency may well be lost when a child has visual recall problems and difficulty with copying.

Some pupils need practice in copying, as they have much of this to do in class. Work on breaking down words into syllables improves both spelling and the fluency of their writing. The teacher may need to stop and assess the legibility of her own writing here – particularly on a board!

A child who does not exert enough pressure on the paper may be encouraged to press harder by using several sheets and seeing on how many the words are clearly indented.

Increasing dictation speeds can be achieved if a tape recorder is used, gradually increasing the speed to familiarise children with the speed generally used by a teacher in class.

A pupil should not be relieved entirely of learning the skills of good handwriting, but a useful aid for those reluctant to write is a word-processor. This often has the added advantage of reinforcing correct spelling patterns and giving the satisfaction of well-presented work. The older pupil, or indeed a youngster with poor motor-control and great difficulty with writing, may benefit enormously from learning keyboard skills.

Computers with word-processors, which are now becoming cheaper, can be a very worthwhile investment. Some external exams (GCSE and A-level in UK) allow work to be presented in this way, as do some universities and colleges. In severe cases a scribe may be permitted in these examinations (see page 66).

Every pupil develops his own style and characteristics, which are representative of inner character, according to graphology. It has been suggested that improvement in writing formation is followed by improvement in character. Whether or not this is the case, it is certainly true that there can be a substantial improvement in self-confidence which, in turn, reflects favourably throughout the pupil's work.

Conclusions

The need to fit the help to the pupil concerned, and his particular circumstances, is of great importance. Ideally, a carefully structured programme of help along the lines suggested in this chapter is to be recommended. However, this may be impracticable when an older pupil is on the verge of taking public exams. In such an instance, there may be no time for more than discussing his writing with him and concentrating his attention on the improvement of one or two specific letters, such as the in the following example:

Example J

Once a child is being taught by subject teachers he is often criticised for his poor writing, but seldom given specific pointers to help. Furthermore, there is often no cohesive policy on handwriting at this stage (see Example K).

Example K

> The advantages and disadvantages
> of continuing at and school
>
> The reasons why I would
> like to leave school now
> are because I believe that it would
> be very advantageous to be able
> to start a job now and in two
> years time when my peers
> leave school I will have already
> had two years experience and
> will in a way have a head start
> into the Real World. although
> the is one great disadvantage
> is that I will have no specialized
> qualifications which I may
> well regret when I wish
> to settle down with a
> permanent job. ~~getting~~ Carrying
> on with school or college
> ~~and~~ getting specialized
> qualifications will also
> open up new opportunities
>
> You must improve your handwriting !

Also, he may revert to printing because he feels the end result is neater and less likely to be criticised, and is unaware of the ultimate advantages of keeping to joined writing. Whatever the circumstances, it is important to set realistic goals. The end results may never satisfy a perfectionist, but if it succeeds in the basics of legibility and fluency, attention may then be concentrated on the all-important content of the text which is, after all, the real purpose of writing.

Chapter 9

Sequencing

Sequencing is used in the sense of either doing things or putting things in their correct order. Many people, especially if they are tired, may mistake the order of the alphabet and then be unable to find a word in the dictionary. Everyone, at some time, fails to follow directions and loses his way. But with dyslexic people these problems are not necessarily just slight weaknesses which they can brush off with a laugh; they are often extreme difficulties which leave them particularly vulnerable. The person who can never quite remember whether October comes before or after September is not labouring under the same difficulty as the person who may have no idea of the order of the months at all. The number of dyslexic people who have problems with aspects of sequencing indicates that this is an area which teachers must take into account.

People carry out all sorts of actions in a particular sequence and, by and large, never give it a thought. For example, as children they had to learn to put their clothes on in an accepted order. Not only are meals taken in a recognised series – breakfast, lunch, tea and supper – but the courses of those meals also have their order. Sometimes people who are ill, or very old people, get confused over the sequence of things and incongruous situations result.

Dyslexic people too, for different reasons, experience certain problems relating to sequencing, particularly if language is involved. Although the order of days, months and seasons is routinely dealt with from reception classes upwards, they may have difficulty in learning their order; they usually have difficulty learning mathematical tables (see Example A), just as they find it difficult to get the order of letters in a word correct (see Chapter 7, Spelling).

William, a bright boy of nearly 12 years was asked if he could say his 2 times table. His version is on the following page 115.

Example A

$1 \times 2 = 2$

$2 \times 2 = 4 \ldots$ um $\ldots$

$3 \times 2 = 6$

$4 \times 2 = 9 \ldots$ I think $\ldots$ no! It's 8. Help! I'm muddled up, is it 9 or 8? I can't remember.

$5 \times 2 = 10$

$6 \times 2 = 15$

$7 \times 2 = 18 \ldots$

$8 \ldots 8 \times 2 \ldots = 19 \ldots$ um $\ldots$ er $\ldots$ and $10 \times 2 = 20$. I think I've missed one out there, haven't I?

Drat! $12 \times 2 = 12$, I think $\ldots$ No. $12 \times 2 \ldots = 23$.

With such confusion, it is far better to provide a table-square or some other concrete aid (see Chapter 11, Numeracy).

Sequencing problems are thrown into relief in the special tests devised and administered by educational psychologists; also by the Bangor Dyslexia Test and Aston Index which can be given by teachers. It is useful if teachers can interpret these tests so that the results can supply helpful information for work with a child. Children may be required to match from memory a sequence of patterns or pictures which have been exposed for five seconds. Often they do less well with symbolic tests than with pictures. Nevertheless, it must be appreciated that any test given is one small piece of the jigsaw when looking at the whole problem.

Apart from pronunciation and spelling (for example, **geogaphry**/geography, **chapular**/bachelor), memorising poems, telephone numbers, multiplication tables – and so much other information that the non-dyslexic schoolchild picks up with comparative ease – may only be acquired by the dyslexic child with much practice.

Suggestions for dealing with these problems

Seasons

There is an order in our lives provided by the seasons of the year and most children soon learn their names and which season follows which. But a teacher should not be surprised to be told by a dyslexic child that autumn comes after winter or summer comes before spring. To cause further confusion some children travel from continent to continent and may leave Australia in spring to arrive in Europe when it is autumn.

It is not unusual for teenagers, even of good intelligence, to be unsure of the order of the seasons. A teacher should check that a child understands the meaning of **before** and **after**, but if these are understood, one is left with a problem of sequencing. The name of each season needs to be linked to the weather and some activity at that time of year. A child might draw pictures to reinforce this. Dyslexic children can be so adrift in the ability to sequence that lessons on the seasons in the early days at school will not have had the same impact as with the rest of the class. It has, therefore, to be done again and reinforced in various ways so that the full meaning becomes apparent.

Days of the week

Many dyslexic children live in a kind of limbo-land. Some days when they get up and play they are allowed to continue undisturbed, while on other days there is a shout from the kitchen asking them to **hurry up and get dressed and come down for breakfast,** otherwise they will be late for school. Sometimes children of 8 or 9, and even older, have only a vague idea of the order of the days of the week.

The days may be linked to different activities – no school on Saturday and Sunday, the weekend; back to school on Monday; football or netball on Wednesday; art on Thursday. It is no use reprimanding a child who has no idea of the days of the week for forgetting to bring his football boots on a Wednesday. To him it will be just another day!

Teachers have many good ways of teaching the order of the days, but one successful and simple way is to have seven strips of card with the days written on each (see Example B). The child can then learn to move these into the correct order, and the actual manipulation provides reinforcement. If on the reverse of the cards there is a picture or pattern, the child can check and correct any mistakes. When he can do this several times, it can be left for a while, but it should be done again from time to time as a check.

Example B

Months

The months are usually more of a problem than the days. To begin with, there are nearly twice as many, and second, as they cover a longer span of time, they recur less often and do not provide the same daily practice (see Example C).

Example C

Feu wei

junon

Mart

Aper

May

junn

sdmerd

Octvd

Dermer

January

febuary

martch

april

may

June

July

augousi

september

November

Dicember

Sean is 11 years old, intelligent but very withdrawn and timid. His mother had been trying to get help for him for years.

This was written by a 15-year-old of average intelligence. He had learnt the order of the months but often May or October is omitted, even when the order of the other months is correct.

Again, slips of paper with the individual months will help the pupil to get accustomed to the correct order. Certain peculiarities may be noted. The two months ending in **uary** go together; the short names – March, April, May and June – come in a group. (April showers bring forth May flowers!) That may help with the first six months. June and July are often confused, so it is a good idea to make a break after June. The second six are usually where the greatest difficulties arise. However, the initial letters of July, August, September, October and November spell JASON, and these may then be known as the JASON months. This seems to provide a useful clue and leaves only December, the month of Christmas, for the very end.

Unless the order of months is mastered, an adult in a job may find himself in a difficult situation. Should a customer ask, for instance, if he can finish some work by April, he will be unable to give a realistic answer, and the customer could well be irritated at his apparent inefficiency and vagueness.

Alphabet

Learning the alphabet is essential in order to look up words in dictionaries or names in telephone directories. Many children pick it up from their early alphabet books or from the alphabet letters on the classroom wall. The dyslexic child, however, often has great difficulty remembering the sequence of twenty-six letters, so this should be checked even with teenagers or adults.

Some children respond to learning the alphabet by singing it and some through rhythm, pausing after **G**, **N** and **U**. Some are helped by having these four groups in different colours. If each letter is on a piece of card in the colour of its group, the colours will be a clue to correct grouping. Children may learn a group of letters at a time. If, in due course, these letters are placed in a semi-circle in front of them, they have the feeling of being surrounded by the alphabet (see Example D). They can then see the letters in relation to one another, where the middle of the alphabet comes and which letters come together.

Example D

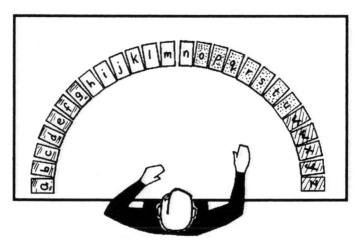

With no mental picture of the alphabet or feeling for its order, these children usually have to start from the beginning until they come to the letter they want. Having learnt the alphabetical sequence, they then need to practise this in the form of being asked: 'Which comes first, L or G?' and 'Which half of the alphabet does K come in? and T?' and so on. In addition, with the alphabet letters in a semi-circle, a letter may be removed while the children shut their eyes; then they are asked if they can spot which letter is missing.

It is useful to remember, when looking up words, that the letters E, M and S indicate the quarters of the dictionary. Not only do children have to learn the alphabetical sequence of letters in order to look up words in dictionaries or names in telephone directories, but they need to be shown

1 that the two words in bold print at the top of pages refer to the first and last words in bold print listed on that page, and
2 that the second, third and fourth letters of each word are in alphabetical order as well.

A retired surgeon, wanting to telephone the family doctor because his wife had had a fall, had to enlist the help of a neighbour to find the doctor's telephone number. It is over this kind of thing that dyslexic people get confused; their underlying weakness becomes apparent from time to time, especially in times of stress and long after they seem to have mastered this difficulty. The same uncertainty can arise when looking up words in a dictionary. No doubt this will have been taught to the class but, again, some will need extra reinforcement. Without it, they will have a sense of inadequacy and lack of confidence. And all dyslexic people need to refer constantly to a dictionary! It has been known for them just to flick over the pages in the hope that they will come across the word they are looking for!

Time

Telling the time is another aspect of sequencing. This can be very confusing for some dyslexic people. For instance, an intelligent 15-year-old girl with faulty reading and appalling spelling admitted that she had only recently learnt to tell the time. (She still had no idea of the order of the months.) For those with severe difficulty, an activity called 'Walking the clock' can be done on the playground or school hall floor. It helps children to visualise the clock face if they 'walk' it. Allow them to set up cones marked as 12, 3, 6 and 9 in the correct positions. Children should be able to do this for themselves and know that 6 is opposite 12 and 3 opposite 9. Then they need to fill in between 12, 3, 6 and 9. Once this is familiar, leave the numbers off all the cones except 12. Can they go to 6? 9? 1? 11? (Reinforce this by playing clock patience, which requires the same skill.) Can they fill in the numbers on a blank clock face on paper? If yes, now teach o'clock. The harder concepts of 5 past, 10 past, and 5 to, 10 to, and so on need to be walked again, starting at 12 every time if necessary, counting forwards to half past, and then counting forwards but moving backwards from 12, calling aloud each minute – 1 minute to, 2 minutes to, ... 5 minutes to, 10 minutes to and so on. After half past, they learn that they are looking to the next hour. It is better to teach the 'past' initially and only when this is established, move on to the 'to'. Teaching both at once compounds the confusion.

The teacher needs to be prepared to provide detailed explanations of fractions, such as a half and quarter, which may have been familiarly used without their real meanings being appreciated. An added complication is that there are various ways of telling the time, like 7.15 and quarter past seven.

Having eventually sorted out the first twelve hours, children now learn the twenty-four-hour clock; these times become more meaningful when related to cookers and video recorders, where children are used to seeing four digits. They can be told that these only show what hours and minutes have passed, for example, 19:50 and 06:45 (as opposed to 20 to 9 which looks forward in time). Relating this to an analogue clock is perplexing, as the numbers on the clock-face do not correspond to the hours. It is only by constant practice that the difficulty is overcome.

Time and sequence of events is another area worth exploring. It is not enough just to be able to tell the time; it also has to be related to the day's events – at what time people generally begin the day, eat meals and go to bed and so on. Estimating the amount of time for certain activities, such as how to be punctual for appointments, enables dyslexic people to lead more ordered lives – as well as those around them!

Concept of time

Let children guess when a minute has passed. Using sand-timers they can, for example, see how many times they can write a word in a minute in order to get the idea of that length of time. Longer periods of time can be related to an activity such as walking across the hall. They could then consider how long it takes for break, for a lesson, how long it takes to half-time in a football match or their favourite TV programme.

Poetry, plays, telephone numbers

Learning poetry by heart or character parts for a play may involve auditory and/or visual sequencing, as does the recall of telephone numbers.

A dyslexic child could spend hours vainly trying to learn a poem set for homework. To remember the word sound-patterns or visualise the words in the correct order of even a short poem can be of such difficulty that teachers may well believe that no effort at all has been made to learn it. Some children find it easier if the poem is recorded on tape, and even learn while they are moving, walking or cycling.

Music

The need for the correct sequencing of notes when reading music often prevents a dyslexic child from learning an instrument. He may be musical and even be able to play by ear, but to follow the score from left to right when his hands are often moving from right to left, as when playing a piano, is sometimes too muddling. An instrument with a single clef may prove easier.

Sequencing of actions

Tying shoe-laces and ties demands actions in a recognised order which many dyslexic children find very difficult. They are often to be seen with shoe-laces trailing. Fortunately for some, Velcro has enabled this problem to be bypassed. Dressing also requires putting on clothes in an acknowledged sequence as well as the right way round (orientation), and more thought has to be given to this than by the non-dyslexic child. Consequently, dressing after PE or swimming may be a slow process which, in turn, may cause a teacher irritation if the reason is not understood.

Reading and spelling

The main areas where sequencing problems are noticed are reading and spelling. Something has already been mentioned about this in Chapter 2, Ears, eyes and IQs, Chapter 6, Reading, and Chapter 7, Spelling, but it is worth noting again under the heading of sequencing. The inability to get letters in their correct order when either reading or writing is a major aspect of dyslexia, and what is read can easily be altered as a result. Similarly, words in sentences may be processed in the wrong order and this, too, can affect the sense, e.g. **He understood the railway timetable at Waterloo./He stood under the railway timetable at Waterloo.** The same problem may also be reflected in a dyslexic child's speech, for example, **loud speaker/speak louder.**

These kinds of mistakes bring to mind the Rev. W. A. Spooner, who was, according to an eminent contemporary, known not only for what became called spoonerisms but also for his bizarre spelling.

There may be problems in the sequencing of events as well. Tenses of verbs may vary from present to past in the same sentence; anachronisms of time may appear and the natural order of actions may be muddled as if nothing had been planned. A dyslexic student often needs detailed instruction on simple past, present and future tenses, and on syntax (the way in which words are put together to form clauses or sentences), in order to be able to write in a consistent tense. Children may learn that there are various tenses in other languages, but be unaware that the same principles apply in English.

The kind of training indicated on pages 127–8 helps dyslexic children who have difficulty in following instructions or directions. Additional practice may be given with the aid of simple maps, and more is written on this subject in Chapter 10, Orientation.

Suggested games and equipment

1   Games like **I went to market and bought ...** , or **I had a birthday and was given ...** , where each child repeats what has gone before and adds one more item (sometimes alphabetically), help to train the ability to sequence auditorily too. Accurate repetition of sentences given by a teacher, or groups of nonsense words, is work towards the same goal.

2   Learning Development Aids (LDA) produce cards specifically to give practice in training visual sequencing and spatial concepts. There are several boxes of cards covering a variety of sequences. The object of the exercise is to increase the pupil's ability to sequence accurately and recall material presented visually. This is critical to the development of:

   • reading – predicting outcome;
   • comprehension;
   • writing – correct sequencing of letters and words;
   • number – processing and using numbers in sequence;
   • problem-solving – ability to plan in steps.

It also stimulates and develops the ability to think in terms of time sequences. This helps children to become aware of the importance of putting things in their correct order. Accurate letter- and word-sequencing can then be encouraged by sorting jumbled words to make sentences. This enables them to become more aware of the need for correct sequencing of letters and words when writing. Training in sentence-structure can be provided with words on different coloured cards for subject, verb, link words, adjective, etc., and the result must make sense.

3   Learning Development Aids also produce dominoes which train accurate sequencing of letters, including blends, to make words.

4   A variety of workbooks provide useful training in alphabetical sequencing, the sequencing of actions in pictures as related to a story, and the correct ordering of sentences to make up a story.

5   Tracking exercises develop an ability to sequence the alphabet, to perceive letter clusters and to train left-to-right eye movement (see Chapter 2, Ears, eyes and IQs).

6   Computer programs are available which give children practice in sequencing words within a sentence, and sentences within a story, as well as pictorial sequencing, such as Word Shark.

7   Further practice can be given by asking a child to tell a story that he has heard or seen on TV. He then has to select incidents in the order that they have happened to relate the story logically. Recording this on a cassette may heighten his awareness of logical order.

Conclusions

It is all too easy to assume, for example, that a child of 10 or 12 is familiar with the months from January to December and to adopt a scornful tone, or show surprise, if this is not so. It is also easy to assume that such everyday matters will be quick and easy to teach when, in reality, a dyslexic person of even high intelligence may need detailed multi-sensory instruction and reinforcement over a period of time before becoming familiar with them.

Improved confidence in one area often reflects through to others, quite apart from the fact that sequencing has an essential link with reading, writing and spelling.

If a pupil is a poor reader and bizarre speller, teachers, even in secondary schools, would be well advised to look for the wider implications of the problems of sequencing which so often accompany the reading and spelling difficulty. In this way the social skills mentioned in this chapter would be improved and the day-to-day life of the dyslexic person made easier.

Chapter 10

Orientation

Orientation is applied in this context to spatial relationships, and sequencing has to do with order. It is therefore evident that there is no clear line of demarcation.

A lack of order and a lack of awareness of relationship of how matters are interrelated so often seems to be a factor when looking at the needs of a dyslexic child. So much of our lives is governed by order and sequence that it is easy to take for granted an in-built awareness of various basic concepts, many of which are merely arbitrary conventions. An ability to relate both objects and events in context is also a prerequisite to analysing situations and problems later.

Perceptual learning is a very complicated process, and it is recognised that normal development takes a child step by step through this. Babies learn by touch and grow aware of feelings such as warmth, coldness, softness and hardness. Later, they see objects and gradually learn to discriminate them from their background. Some children are slow to develop fully in this area and, although they may have no difficulty when faced with physical objects, they are at a loss later when asked to pick a letter out of a word or a word from within a sentence. In practical terms this comes back to difficulty in copying from a book or board, difficulty in looking up words in a list or dictionary, difficulty in looking up an index or telephone number and difficulty in finding the place again if momentarily distracted while reading.

Later still a child learns that an object does not change simply because he sees it from another angle, and that a cup, for instance, remains a cup in whatever position it is placed.

Example A

A bag of 3D alphabet letters enables children to recognise them through touch. Pupils can roll out plasticine or Playdoh and make their own 3D alphabet as well – this will also have the effect of making their handwriting easier because of the exercise. Some will need to make or handle these letters frequently until they can be recognised as 2D shapes on paper. A child may readily accept this, but then be introduced to our alphabet, in which it is imperative that each letter is always reproduced facing a particular way. He may find it very difficult to perceive that **b** and **d** are not one and the same, and when he does understand that they are two different letters there is the problem of remembering which is which (see Fig. 2, page 71).

Others may find spatial relationships difficult. This is primarily a matter of relating objects to the child himself. Second, there are problems in relating the position of one object to another object. In practical terms this can make for difficulties such as knowing where on a page to draw the margin or to begin to write, or where to begin to read, how and in which direction to form letters, as well as the difficulty with the order of the letters or syllables in a word. Problems with spatial ability and directional awareness are very pertinent to maths work (see Chapter 11, Numeracy).

Furthermore, if the child is confused about the meaning of words describing spatial concepts, his comprehension will suffer. For instance, if he is unsure of the terms **left** and **right** or does not know the difference between **further** and **nearer**, he may be unable to carry out a series of tasks correctly and may do the opposite to what the teacher has just told him. Physical exercises can be a miserable activity for such a child as he vainly struggles to follow instructions and do the same as the others. He may be putting his hands up when the rest are putting theirs down; he is probably turning to the left when the others are turning right, or moving forwards when he should be going backwards. In the end he may resort to copying his fellows and usually be picked out in class because he is a movement or two behind them. Some army cadets on parade, when, for instance, consistently turning left instead of right, have been found to have literacy problems.

There are two factors to be taken into account. First, there is a *language-based* difficulty. The problem seems to be one of terminology in remembering, for instance, the label 'left' as being attached to that direction, but the child is still able to get himself from one place to another without becoming lost. Second are those children – a smaller group, but a significant one – who appear *totally confused in time and space* and may be found wandering the corridors in search of, perhaps, the school office if sent on an errand. Their problem may go unnoticed because pupils usually move around the school in groups. All teachers can bring to mind the child who appears to live in a world of his own and, as the saying goes, is on another planet.

Suggestions for dealing with these problems

As with other aspects of dyslexia, it often helps the pupil to discuss the difficulty in broad terms and to do this in the way most suited to his intelligence and maturity. Older pupils are usually most relieved to find that they are not alone in being late to learn to read, to learn the alphabet or tell the time, to follow directions to a particular place or to read a map. It can be an enormous relief to them to know that their teacher does not automatically expect that they should be familiar with these things. Equally, it can be reassuring to know that others have similar or perhaps even greater difficulties and that these are not considered insurmountable.

Selected sheets from Puzzle Books and Fun Books (usually obtainable from local stationers) are extremely useful for younger children and often a readily acceptable form of homework. These give practice in picking out objects from a background, grouping objects, matching shapes and in a variety of useful activities. A child who struggles with these activities often seems to struggle with literacy.

There is also graded material produced specifically to help with such difficulties (see pages 122–3). Different approaches suit different pupils, and teachers will need to evaluate and select appropriate material from the ever-widening choice available. It is helpful for class teachers to link up and discuss this with dyslexia specialists.

Size

An early concept to tackle could be that of size. **Small, large** and the degrees of these are a good starting point. Objects can be related to one another in terms of size: for example, a **large** book and a **small** book and a **smaller** book; and then in relation to imagined objects, like a **pin** and an **elephant**. Some children may have difficulty imagining or visualising these differences. Finally, it is helpful to use the terms in an abstract sense and explain the use of comparative and superlative; for example, **bad, worse, worst**. Games to find the greatest number of words indicating large or small can also serve to expand children's vocabulary and give them an awareness of the alternatives open to them when writing. This improves their general comprehension too; such words are **huge, vast, enormous, extensive** *or* **tiny, minute, miniature, microscopic**.

Shapes

Consideration of various shapes follows on well from comparison of sizes. Depending on the age and abilities of the pupils, some or all of the following shapes may be brought to their attention, **round, circle, sphere, oval, triangle, cone, quadrangle, hexagon, polygon, cube, pyramid, cylinder**.

These often seem particularly difficult to remember (see Chapter 11, Numeracy). Another group which may be usefully discussed are **short, wide, broad, narrow, long** and perhaps **perpendicular, diagonal, vertical, horizontal, parallel** and **taper.** Accurate terminology is essential for the written word when there can be no gestures to support the meaning! Children are introduced to many of these in early Maths lessons, but some do not grasp them at this stage and they will need re-teaching at later stages.

Spatial relationships

Prepositions or connectives are words which refer to the relative position of one object to another. There must be a relationship or connection between the objects. This is an enormous group of words, and practice with them needs to be related both to pupils themselves and objects in relation to one another. Words such as **near, far, to, from, by, with, beside, along, across, before, behind, amongst, beyond, over, under, around, between, after, beneath, about, close to** and **in front of,** may cause a dyslexic child – and adult – particular confusion. Teachers should be aware of this possible confusion when using such terms – especially the terms **before** and **after** when applied to spelling, and sometimes to reading, and indeed even for paragraph references. For instance, in spelling conventions when a **Y** is changed to the letter **I** for plural suffixes, a child is asked to look at the letter *before* the **Y**; it may then be discovered that he was looking at the letter *after*, because he interpreted the concept differently. It should never be taken for granted that pupils have mastered these concepts, however basic they may seem.

A simple sketch, such as Example B (page 128), is one of the easiest ways to work through these words. Questions such as, **'How many ducklings are there behind the duck?'** usually show where any uncertainties lie in the meanings of these words. A typical error is a pupil pointing to the front view of the bird when asked to find something in front of something else.

Left and right

Uncertainty over left and right is often present. Apart from confusion over following directions, margins may be drawn on the right-hand side of the page, or there may be confusion with number lines (see Chapter 11, Numeracy) when counting on and back. Many dyslexic children teach themselves by referring to a scar, the wrist on which they wear a watch or their writing hand. The trouble with this reasoning is that it often breaks down at moments of stress. This may happen, for instance, in a driving test, when panic takes over and they are left completely uncertain which way to turn and wildly trying to collect their thoughts. Some kind

Example B

of memory tag in the car to indicate left and right can be helpful. When coming to a roundabout in the UK it may be useful to remember that traffic on the Right has the Right of way, traffic on the Left gets Left behind.

However, children must be sure of their own left and right before they can learn what is left and right of them. A good way to start is for pupils to make physical movements so that they feel the raising of the left hand, or tapping of the right knee and so on. Simple requests can gradually become complex by asking them to do things like touching the right ear with the left hand. Even if a student assures you that he knows the difference between left and right, unless this has become automatic, an unexpected instruction may leave him confused.

Another useful exercise is to have about six piles of pencils or other suitable objects and ask the children, '**How many pencils are in the pile on the left of the smallest pile?**' progressing to '**Move two pencils from the pile second on the right to that third from the left**'. Here, an awareness can grow that it is possible for an object to be left of one thing and right of another at the same time. The terms convey a relationship in space between person and object or objects themselves.

A point which usually needs careful explanation is that when facing somebody, that person's left and right are the reverse way on. One can convey the idea by asking a group of children to raise their right hands and to notice, for example, that these are on the side nearest to the window and then, keeping them raised, ask them to face the other way and see if their raised hands are still on the side nearest to the window. Still sitting opposite the teacher, the children are asked to point to the teacher's left hand with their right hands. Therefore, their own left and right sides are constant but the general concept depends on a relationship.

A Roamer, Turtle or Pixie (PIP) are useful devices which can be programmed by a child pressing buttons or a teacher can pre-programme a course of directions. The Roamer can be used in the hall or playground.

Example C

If a pre-school child has immature body awareness and does not improve, he will have trouble later in his school life with topics such as geometry and laying out information correctly.

Familiarity will only come with practice, and it is important to vary this. A sketch of a person can be drawn by child or teacher and coloured in parts in odd moments or at the end of a lesson. For instance, his left shoe could be red and his right knee-patch yellow. When completed, the exercise can take the form of questions like, **'Which hand holds the dog's lead?'** and **'What colour is his left shoe?'**.

A similar sketch, Example D, showing a line of people, can be used in the same way as the piles of pencils. The use of colour does much to enliven these sketches, and further questions can be put like, **'What colour hair has the person on the right of the girl with long hair?'** and **'How many people are on the left of the bald man?'**.

Example D

A sketch of a classroom seating plan can be given. The teacher's desk may be in any one of the four numbered positions, and it must be clearly understood that children in this class all sit facing the teacher (see Example E). It may be necessary to start by actually walking and touching the positions of desks and pupils and then go to a 2D drawing of them.

Example E

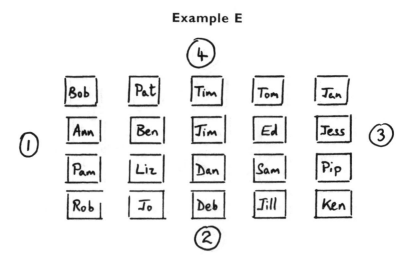

Questions can then be asked:

If, for instance, the teacher is at position 4 –

Who is on Ed's right?

How many people are on Jo's left?

How many people are behind Sam? . . . Do we mean directly behind or further back in the room?

Who is in front of Ben? and so on.

Example F shows the making of drawings using squared paper. A starting point is made, and children are told to move two squares to the left, or one down, and so on. They do not know what their pictures will be until they have finished and then they can fill in details, such as the eyes and the nose. This exercise can also be used when teaching the words **vertical, horizontal** and **diagonal**.

Example F

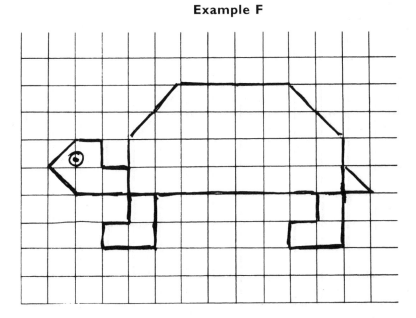

The most advanced and practical exercise is to use a map (see Example G). This may be as simple or complex as desired. Places need not be labelled, and cut-out symbols may be used for non-readers. Alternatively, the names of streets might reinforce spellings recently learnt, like, for example, **ee** or **ar** letter combinations if they need further practice.

Example G

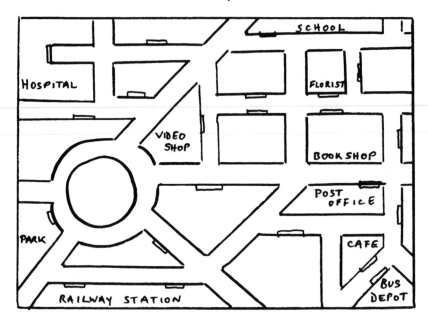

Children can work in pairs or groups while a story is told and they must follow the events, noting whether they are going to the left or right. Perhaps they start at the station and are to make their way to see a friend in hospital. They find it is not visiting time so they go to purchase some flowers and a book. They realise they have left their money somewhere and have to re-trace their steps. Further complications can be made with the use of one-way streets.

Orienteering, starting with simple directions, is an excellent activity for dyslexic people.

It is important not only for children to follow directions, but to be able to give them as well – a lesson that would be of value to everybody if one is to judge from the answers given when asking the way in a strange town! This often proves more difficult if they are making up the story at the same time. The spoken language aspect is important, and the ability to sequence ideas and words into well-constructed sentences is required for National Curriculum targets. It is also a prerequisite to success in writing. Indeed, oral games where questions must be answered with a full sentence can be difficult. The practice of putting the events of a story logically can be useful, as this is something that dyslexic children often find particularly hard.

Geography requirements in the National Curriculum suggest the use of a standard local map. Symbols on an Ordnance Survey map open up a whole new area for teaching and discussion. **Port** and **starboard, near-** and **off-side** are also worth teaching as terms commonly used in sailing, horse-riding or driving cars.

Points of the compass

It is helpful first to discuss the use of a compass, and the fact that the needle swings to point to the north. Magnetic north and true north may provide an interesting point for discussion. The **N** for Needle and North can be related. Then the need for consistency in maps may be mentioned and the fact that the north, being important and our key point, is put at the top of the page. South sinks to the bottom – emphasis on the **S** for South and Sinks. The next most important line goes across the page and it is simple to write the word **WE** to place **W**est and **E**ast correctly. One might expect a dyslexic child sometimes to reverse the letters of this word, but fortunately it rarely seems to happen! Many children use the mnemonic Never Eat Shredded Wheat, which they read in a clockwise direction, to remember the four points of the compass.

Example H

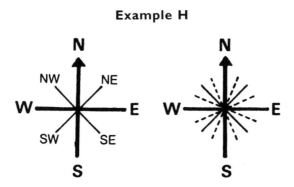

It can then be learnt that the point midway between two points simply takes the two names together, but the more important name must go first. North/south were learnt first and determine the order, so we have north-east, south-west and so on. This is usually readily grasped and, following the same principle, a sixteen-point compass presents no problem. Again, the point takes the two names together with the more important first. Hence north-north-east, west-south-west, and so on. Do not attempt to introduce more than one of these steps at a time. Secure foundations taken slowly undoubtedly help retention, as does the revision needed before each new point.

A demonstration using a globe illustrates further the point that places are either east, west, north or south of other places. India, for example, cannot be classified as to the east if one is Chinese! Germany is in the west even though east of the United Kingdom. The political use of west and east, however, may increase the difficulty in comprehending that it is all a matter of relationship; particularly when we even have Middle East and Far East!

It could be helpful to have the four points of the compass pinned up accurately in the classroom or painted on the playground so that children can see the relation to the sun, especially in the winter when the days are short.

Example I shows a simple form of map for early exercises on direction. Again, there is the opportunity to practise the sequencing of events in a story which can be invented to fit any particular interest or current topic. Children can be asked at some point to imagine themselves on top of the hill and to describe what they might see if they were to face any given direction; also, for instance, whether the sun would be in their eyes if they were facing west at midday, or, if facing south whether the sun would be on their right or left in the early morning.

Example I

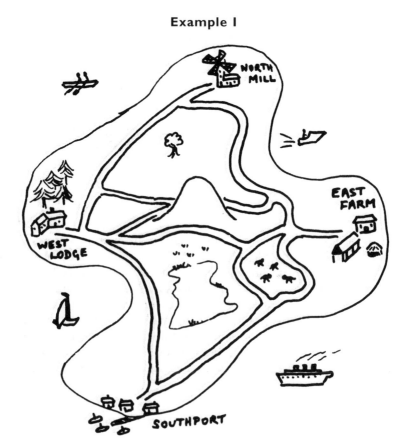

Example J gives a more advanced map on which they can learn to use map references. In order to read grid references properly some are helped if they are told they must **walk along the passage before going upstairs** to remind them that the first reference is on the horizontal and the second on the vertical axis.

Example J

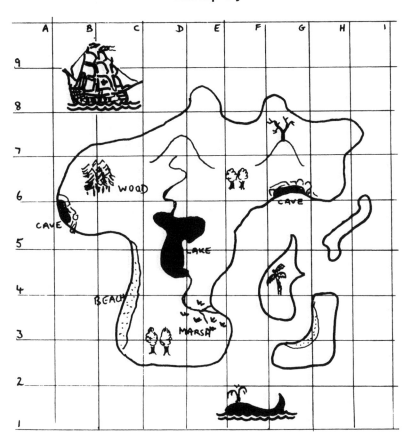

A treasure map with cut-out symbols to represent pirate ships is always popular, and can also be labelled to reinforce particular spellings. The reluctant writer may be persuaded to write a few sentences to go with his map. Colour gives more scope too in the use of the map. Pupils are generally keen to draw a map or sketch for themselves, but drawing one to precise instructions, either spoken or written, is another good exercise.

The old maxim of **little and often** in class is best applied to work on problems of orientation and sequencing as, of course, it is with most teaching. It is often easier to remember to include these exercises in the lessons of younger pupils. However, this aspect of dyslexia is important and should always be considered whatever the age and stage of the pupil.

Conclusions

Many of the areas of orientation which pose great difficulties for the dyslexic child have been mentioned. Some dyslexic children will have difficulty in several areas, and the difficulties themselves will vary in severity according to the degree of dyslexia and the intellectual ability of the individual concerned. However, many people who are not dyslexic have individual idiosyncrasies about such things as right and left or reading maps, and it is acknowledged that these difficulties are not peculiar to dyslexic children.

However, the incidence of these difficulties related to dyslexia is so high that we cannot afford to treat them lightly. It can be extremely depressing for someone, whose confidence may already be eroded by his literacy problems, to be unable to find his way, follow simple directions or tell the time as others around him do without hesitation. The more that assurance and confidence is eroded, the greater is the risk of secondary psychological problems, such as withdrawal or delinquency.

Chapter 11

Numeracy

It would be remarkable if many of the children who have difficulties with literacy skills did not also have trouble with mathematics. This takes us back to our innate learning differences.

As with difficulties in reading, it is important to pause and consider the reasons for the particular difficulties that the child is experiencing. Is there a receptive language problem, a difficulty with sequencing and orientation (order and direction), a weakness in transferring information to long-term memory and/or a maths phobia?

Many class teachers feel far less sure of themselves when helping children with weak skills in mathematics. Some who are natural mathematicians find it hard to understand how basic concepts are not readily absorbed. Many others have never felt quite secure with maths and tend to teach particular tried and tested methods that happened to suit their own learning style. This lack of flexibility in approach, or extra lessons which consist of **more of the same**, can aggravate children's feelings of failure and convince them that they will never be able to do maths.

Indeed, there are a number of children who do not expect to succeed as they have so often heard one or other parent stating firmly that they **were never any good at maths**. A weakness with numeracy skills can often be laughed off by an adult and carries nothing like the stigma of weak literacy skills.

A chapter in a book of this nature can do little more than touch upon some of the difficulties to be found in such a complex subject but, it is hoped, it will encourage teachers to look closely at the particular reasons that are, perhaps, causing the problems for an individual. Many of our ideas have been gleaned from work done by Dr Steve Chinn and Professor Mahesh Sharma.

Broadly speaking, people lie somewhere on a continuum between two types of learning categories. These are described by Dr Steve Chinn as the inchworm and grasshopper. The inchworm is described alternatively by Professor Mahesh Sharma as having a *quantitative* approach. This means that the inchworm type needs to progress step by step through the parts of a problem to the final solution. The grasshopper, on the other hand, makes intuitive leaps, often achieving the correct solution, but unable to explain how he reached it. This is the *qualitative* approach, and these are the pupils who work from the whole to the parts of a problem. Children may not necessarily fit clearly into one or other of these categories, but they are useful guidelines to remind teachers of the different ways in which people function.

Inevitably, every classroom will have pupils from each extreme and in between. If a teacher presents everything in the quantitative way there are going to be children who miss out, and vice versa. Many textbooks for primary schoolchildren work very much in the step-by-step, sequential way, and the qualitative pupils may end up, quite wrongly, believing that they have no ability in maths. Both types need consideration and lessons should be planned accordingly.

Pupils who can access both styles will be better problem solvers and more able to check their answers reliably. The National Numeracy Strategy encourages a flexible approach to learning maths and thus to problem solving.

Language

Maths has its own language, and this can be the root of many problems. General mathematical terminology with words like **perimeter, value, equals** may be unfamiliar. It is interesting to ask a class to define the word **equals** and see the many different replies, perhaps most commonly that it means **answer**. These words all need to be clearly understood before they can be used in calculations. Many of these words are not used in other contexts and, therefore, are not constantly practised, so their meanings often seem to elude the memory. However, mathematical words are sometimes used in different contexts which can cause more confusion; for example, **it all adds up** may occur in a conversation and be emphasising a negative attitude.

To complicate matters further, one single mathematical process can be described with a wide variety of terms; for instance, **multiply, times, product, of** or **add, increase, plus, sum, total**. The representation of these groups are × or +, symbols that are extremely alike, particularly for the pupil with spatial difficulties.

Numbers, too, are confusing in themselves, in that they may be absolute or have a relative value. Hence, in 6000, 600, 60, 6, 0.6, ⅙, 6% the actual digit **6** conveys very different meanings.

The National Numeracy Strategy is encouraging more practical maths as well as mere sums, which means many of the problems are set in words. Therefore, the child may have difficulty in:

1   decoding the print to read the problem; and
2   his comprehension might be such that he still remains uncertain about what working he needs to do; or
3   he may have difficulty in the computation of the figures themselves.

The pupil may have no problem with informal mathematical language; for example,

92 take away 39

but be confused by the formal language and particularly the reverse order of

subtract 39 from 92.

Making up number stories and translating from numbers to words is as vital as the more usual process of problems in which we turn the words to numbers. The type of number story given by the child often gives an indication of the approach which suits him best. For example,

Given the numbers 5, 7, 2, and asked to turn these into a sum, the inchworm may say, **There were 5 people on the bus, 7 more got on and 2 got off. How many were left?**

The grasshopper is more likely to see the problem overall and recognise that the sum of 5 and 2 is 7 and use this fact in his illustration.

The continuity and flexibility of language and approach are extremely important, and it is essential that the teacher is aware of which maths methods and language the child has experienced, and can expect to experience, as he progresses through the school. Does the language used by the teacher match the textbooks, and – of utmost importance – is the help being given at home perhaps adding further to the confusion? Close liaison in this area is extremely important, and meetings between class teachers and, if appropriate, with parents, for discussion of consistency of methods are to be recommended.

The child should be taught to form the habit of always checking his answer against the question when he has finished the calculation. Is his answer possible, sensible or ludicrous? The value of learning the skills of estimation cannot be too strongly stressed, although many find estimation very difficult, particularly if they have a poor sense of place value. Good visual recall for holding figures in the mind's eye makes this far easier although, of course, this may be the main area of difficulty for many dyslexic children.

Mental arithmetic

Mental arithmetic often poses particular problems for dyslexic children, especially in the demands it makes on short-term memory. They have difficulty in retaining the information given in the question in order to extract the sense and process the answer – all within the short time allowed. Plenty of practice is needed in jotting down the **key number** and appropriate mathematical sign from the question to help overcome this.

Sequencing

Problems with orientation and sequencing (direction and order) are obviously going to have considerable bearing on layout, place value and subsequent computation. When marking a child's work it is important to check the reason for the errors. For example, the pupil may have added perfectly correctly

$$35 + 41 = 76$$

but may have miscopied the sum, which should have been 35 + 14, and not be aware of the reason for the mistake.

Counting in sequence is difficult for some, and time spent on establishing a proficiency in counting both forwards and backwards is a prerequisite to establishing number bonds and a sense of number patterns.

Pupils should be able to count up *and back* in ones, twos (many find this quite easy with even numbers but much more difficult with odd numbers), tens and fives. Furthermore, they should be able to do this starting at any number, although they may find this disproportionately challenging. As they count they should be encouraged to try to visualise the number, for example:

71, 73, 75, 77, 79, 81, etc.

93, 91, 89, 87, 85, etc.

13, 23, 33, 43, 53, 63, etc.

117, 107, 97, 87, 77, etc.

These same sequencing difficulties can become apparent with calculator work. The child may be well aware of the required mathematical step but press the buttons in the wrong order.

$32\overline{)365}$ becomes $32 \div 635$.

He may know that the answer is impossible but be quite unable to work out where he went wrong, so he thinks that perhaps the calculator is faulty! A calculator may be a tremendous support for some children but they need practice in using it efficiently.

Children with directional confusion have had to learn that they read from left to right. Addition, subtraction and multiplication then work from right to left. But division suddenly reverts to left to right. Further confusion arises with long multiplication, with some learning to multiply by the units first and others by the tens; for example:

$$
\begin{array}{r}
54 \\
\times 32 \\
\hline
108 \\
1620 \\
\hline
1728 \\
\hline
\end{array}
\qquad \text{or} \qquad
\begin{array}{r}
54 \\
\times 32 \\
\hline
1620 \\
108 \\
\hline
1728 \\
\hline
\end{array}
$$

In our experience the former is often easier for a dyslexic child to remember, as there is consistency in the direction of the numbers being used, and insecure learners need consistency.

Number bonds

An awareness of, and facility with, number bonds speeds up workings enormously, but before these are established other strategies may be developed. For instance, to subtract 9, it is simpler to subtract 10 (counting down in tens already being established) and then to add 1. This is far quicker and generally achieved with fewer errors than an attempt to count back 9 on the fingers. Because counting backwards is so difficult, it is surprising how many children have not realised that it is safer, before number bonds are established, to count forwards in subtraction; for example,

12 − 5 . . . do *not* count back on the fingers

12, 11, 10, 9, 8, 7 (possibly stopping at 8 because the 12 was used as the starting point!)

but count *up* from the 5 to 6, 7, 8, 9, 10, 11, 12 which gives 7 fingers.

This possibly arises because early subtraction work has been done with number lines more than actual blocks. However, the quicker a knowledge of number bonds is established, and the less counting on fingers, the better!

| 1 | 2 | 3 | 4 | 5 | 6 | 7 | 8 | 9 | 10 |

To use a number line to work out 4 + 3, the child learns to put his finger on the 4 and count forward 3 places, arriving at the answer 7. Likewise, to work out 7 − 3 he would put his finger on the 7 and count back 3 places to arrive at the answer 4.

Using practical equipment a child should develop a sense of the value of numbers, perhaps using some key facts such as doubles, and work accordingly; for example:

6 + 7 should relate to 6 + 6 + 1, hence 6 + 7 = 12 + 1 = 13

To establish number bonds, the *pattern method* of learning is extremely effective. Frequent inclusion of patterns practised orally, with visual reinforcement, takes very little time and pays great dividends because it is repetitive reinforcement; for instance.

$$8 + 4 = ?$$
$$4 + 8 = ?$$
$$18 + 4 = ?$$
$$14 + 8 = ?$$
$$24 + 8 = ?$$
$$28 + 4 = ? \text{ etc.}$$

By the time each child in the class has answered the question, all will have had the main bond repeated many times, aiding memory.

However, there is a *constant* need to review and practise, and this needs to be borne in mind as children progress up the school – just as a musician needs to practise basic scales long after becoming a competent player. Children who are weak at maths need positive reinforcement of basics over a long period of time, **possibly throughout their schooling, but never at the expense of conceptual development.**

As progress is made and the patterning becomes evident, subtraction facts can also be included; for example:

$$8 + 4 = ? \qquad 8 + ? = 12$$
$$4 + 8 = ? \qquad ? + 4 = 12$$
$$12 - 4 = ?$$
$$12 - 8 = ? \qquad \text{etc.}$$

modelled, for example, with Cuisenaire rods.

Multiplication tables

These are renowned for the problems they can give a dyslexic child (and his parents and teachers) and are probably the cause of more blood, sweat and tears over the years than all other forms of homework and tests.

However, if basic addition facts are known along with number awareness, the key is there when a child realises that multiplication is a quick method of repeated addition. Practical equipment that can be manipulated is essential to establish this. Reversing the process for division seems generally far harder to grasp. Table squares are a good visual aid and, particularly if the child is encouraged to mutter aloud as he works, their use becomes a multisensory learning technique! It is far better for a child to work with a table square and complete a reasonable part of an exercise than to labour over very few sums because he does not know his tables.

It is all too easy for teachers to expect too much. It is normal practice to ask a child: **Please learn your six times table tonight.** It might well be far better to ask the dyslexic child to learn two related facts, possibly with concrete aids; namely:

(1) $2 \times 6 = 12$ and (2) $4 \times 6 = 24$

Check these facts for the next couple of days and then add one or two more. It may sound a long-winded process but often brings a more complete and quicker success in the end, plus a better understanding of number. To keep the revision going and for the teacher to keep track of what has been covered, blank playing-cards are an invaluable aid. On one side write the question, and on the other the answer. If each table is done in a different colour there is a further memory aid; for example:

These can be shuffled, and the child can work with them from either side, self-checking as he goes, or with a partner. Initially, he will be turning the card to see the answer, but as he progresses he will be saying the answer before he turns the card for checking and visual reinforcement. The reverse side can be used for division facts. Therefore, it is possible to cater for the different levels in the class.

Table squares

1	2	3	4	5	6	7	8	9	10
2	4	6	8	10	12	14	16	18	20
3	6	9	12	15	18	21	24	27	30
4	8	12	16	20	24	28	32	36	40
5	10	15	20	25	30	35	40	45	50
6	12	18	24	30	36	42	48	54	60
7	14	21	28	35	42	49	56	63	70
8	16	24	32	40	48	56	64	72	80
9	18	27	36	45	54	63	72	81	90
10	20	30	40	50	60	70	80	90	100

Finger tables

Some children enjoy finger tables and find them useful to get by in a class test, but in the long term they are inefficient because there is no way of reversing the process for division.

Place the hands flat on the table and number them as illustrated:

$8 \times 7 = 56$

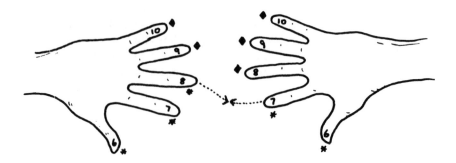

For example, to calculate 8 × 7, connect at the fingertips the 8 on the left hand to the 7 on the right hand. The pupil counts the fingers nearest to himself and including the two touching * = 5. This denotes the tens: 50. The back fingers ◆ 2 on the left and 3 on the right are multiplied together: 2 × 3 = 6 for the units.

Spatial problems

Those with spatial problems often have difficulty in setting out their calculations correctly. A poor understanding of place value and also difficulty in keeping to columns can turn 63.55 + 4 into

$$63.55 \quad \text{or} \quad 63.55$$
$$+ \ 4 \qquad\quad\ \ +4$$

as opposed to

$$63.55$$
$$+4$$

Squared paper is the best on which to work – and preferably the squares should be of a size in which pupils can comfortably write one digit per square. As with written work, clear headings, neat margins, plenty of spacing between workings and the use of a ruler make an enormous difference to the end product, even if the calculations are incorrect! This has to be emphasised right from the beginning. The habit of writing each new step of a calculation immediately *below* the last should also be encouraged. Children who persistently reverse digits, e.g.

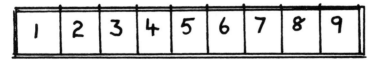

should have a small clue card to check against as they write down their sums.

Exercises in symmetry and the correct use of protractors and measurement of angles are particularly hard for a child with poor spatial and directional awareness. However, for some children these can be areas of success, as they are less dependent on number skills and knowledge.

Practical work

It is well recognised that practical work with concrete aids is a prerequisite to understanding abstract number concepts. All infants spend time manipulating blocks, matching, classifying, weighing, measuring, spending time on pattern recognition, space organisation, dice, playing-cards and other number games.

However, the demands of the curriculum often mean that abstract concepts are being tackled before the child is at the developmental level to cope. Practical understanding of the basic concept of numbers, weight, size and so on must first be established, and concrete aids should have their place in every classroom where there is a child struggling with maths.

There is a wealth of choice of linking bricks, blocks and other materials at our disposal nowadays, and all have their disciples. It is better if individual children can select the materials that work for them. Some experts favour Cuisenaire rods. Certainly, our experience has shown these to be extremely good, particularly as there is the added reinforcement of the constancy of size and colour representing each number. Also, they are small enough for easy manipulation when doing multiplication and other calculations.

Many children find it easier to work with numbers if they first convert them into objects that they can picture in their mind's eye; for example:

8 + 5 = ? is easier to deal with if the child actually says **I have 8 apples and I get 5 more apples so how many apples do I now have?**

This helps with algebra too: **5a** as an unknown abstract is harder to comprehend than **5 apples**. Measurements become more meaningful if they appreciate that the length of a football pitch is approximately 100 m or their own height is 130 cm and so on. This awareness of a sense of number is vital for estimation and for self-checking the answer to a problem.

Board games with dice and many playing-card games improve the child's general facility with numbers, and parents should be encouraged to appreciate the very real value of these. Besides, they have the added value of being fun and developing social co-operation, as well as being disguised work with numbers. Sadly, cultures change and children have less experience with these games today.

Revision

Many children are quick to pick up new concepts and make satisfactory progress through all the exercises in class. However, a couple of weeks later, when they have moved on to a new topic, they appear to have forgotten everything – to their chagrin and the despair of the teacher.

Sometimes a single word or comment is enough to trigger the memory and set them off into the correct sequence of the calculation, but unfortunately this help is not available in examinations!

In order to establish concepts in long-term memory, every new step and concept must be rehearsed immediately. This can be done by always setting aside a few minutes at the end of every lesson for a résumé via oral questions. Ideally, every lesson should begin and end with a quick oral review which should involve *all* the children present. The National Numeracy Strategy also has the benefit of frequent returns to topics, thus helping memory issues. Unfortunately, it does move along at a significant pace.

The teaching needs to be multisensory, with auditory, visual and kinaesthetic senses all being used (see Chapter 7, Spelling). Many children find it helpful to verbalise and **talk** their way through each step of a problem, and this should be encouraged. They should be encouraged to visualise numbers and sums in their mind's eye, to hold a series of digits mentally and perhaps manipulate them. Daily practice of this, along with counting and number bonds, will actually take very little of a teacher's time and can pay enormous dividends.

When a child has made an error it may be necessary to go back to the beginning of the computation when explaining his mistake. He may have done the first steps perfectly well and the teacher is tempted to intervene at the point of error, but many of these children find it difficult to switch into the middle and need to work through *all* the steps each time.

Revision of maths for exams and tests is often difficult. Weekly revision is necessary for success with those who struggle in this subject.

Teachers may find it helpful for each child to keep a **revision book** in which are entered examples of each new topic covered. The left-hand page gives a step-by-step list of instructions, and the right-hand page step-by-step examples. This is particularly important when certain maths schemes and work-cards are used. It is very difficult for a child to find examples needed for revision from his own exercise book, especially as it is unlikely that the questions are also there.

In this revision book each step is explained. Maths terminology is used and cannot be misinterpreted; if the child is encouraged to read out each step, there is additional reinforcement for the memory. Such a book can be kept and added to year by year as the child moves up the school.

For instance, the illustration on page 148 would come after earlier example pages in the revision book, which had already dealt with equivalent fractions, improper fractions and so on. The diagrams below, as well as other diagrams from Ann Henderson's book *Maths for the Dyslexic: A Practical Guide* and the glossary of terms in Vicki Burge's book *Dyslexia – Basic Numeracy*, provide useful ideas for revision.

Addition of fractions – example from a child's revision book

Explanation (including non-mathematical language) Left page	Calculation Right page
Remember: 2 dogs + 4 cats = 2 dogs + 4 cats You can't add them because they are *different* families *but* 2 animals + 4 animals = 6 animals *same* family.	$\dfrac{2}{3} + \dfrac{4}{5}$ Likewise thirds and fifths are different families
The **d**own (**d**enominator) number gives the *family* so we need these to be the same.	
What number do the down numbers both go into? (Check the higher number multiples first.) 15 is the common multiple.	$\dfrac{2}{3} + \dfrac{4}{5}$ 3, 6, 9, 12, 15 : 5, 10, 15 The multiples
What did we do to each down number to change the family?	$\dfrac{2}{3} + \dfrac{4}{5}$ $\times 5 \qquad \times 3$ $\qquad 15$
Whatever we did to the bottom number, we *must* do to the top.	$\begin{array}{cc} \times 5 & \times 3 \\ \dfrac{2}{15} + & \dfrac{4}{5} \end{array}$
They are now the same family (equivalent fractions) so we can add the numerators.	$\dfrac{10}{15} + \dfrac{12}{15}$
Remember The **d**own number (**d**enominator) tells us how many we need to make a whole one. The top number (numerator) tells us how many we have.	$\dfrac{22}{15}$
Is the top number bigger than the down number? YES! *So we have a whole number, and a bit left over*	$\dfrac{22}{15}$
How many times does the **d**own (**d**enominator) go into the top – and how many are left over?	$1\dfrac{7}{15}$
Can we **cancel** (simplify)? (Is there a number that goes into top and bottom of fraction?)	NO Ans. = $1\dfrac{7}{15}$

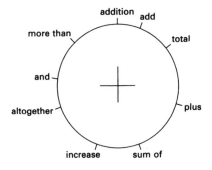

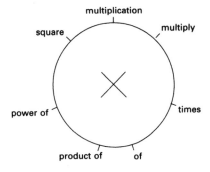

Suggestions for class teachers

1. For early computation, the child should always label the place values of HTU and then be taught that he *must*, before each sum, say

   Which side do I begin?

   Then for addition/subtraction/multiplication

   Top – *sign* – bottom

	HTU	
Therefore	34	**I begin with the units**
	−17	**Top = 4**
	———	**Sign = Take away**
	———	**Bottom = 7**

   I can't do it – so I must go next door and fetch 10, etc.

   He should continue to say **Top-sign-bottom** for each part of the sum, and this helps those inclined to switch from subtraction to addition halfway through the sum, and those who instinctively wish to **take** the smaller number from the larger, regardless of position.

2   less than    greater than

transformed into crocodile jaws which *must* be at their widest for the bigger number

6 < 8   8 > 6

3   Fractions always require a great deal of language work before they are understood. The understanding of a fraction being **one of the** *equal* **parts of a whole** *must* be established.

So many children, when asked **What is a fraction?** reply **It's a half** or **It's a bit of something**. Fractions require not only language but conceptual work. Consider:

The smaller the fraction the bigger the number of parts, which is the reverse of normal counting ½ > ¹⁄₂₀. Having established this you have to come to terms with ⅝ > ½. Fraction strips are far clearer than circles to demonstrate the understanding of equivalent fractions, particularly with different colours being used to mark the equivalent lines; e.g.

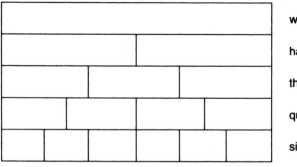

$$\therefore \quad \frac{1}{2} \ = \ \frac{2}{4} \ = \ \frac{3}{6}$$

$$\frac{1}{3} \ = \ \frac{2}{6}$$

4   Arrows for multiplication of fractions to remind the pupil of the cancelling step

5   Some who find it difficult to convert different units of measurement, e.g. cm → m or mm → cm because they are uncertain whether they must divide or multiply, and by how many, find this chart form easier to deal with.

th	h	t	u	tnth	hth	thth
kilo-	hecta-	deca-	metre	deci-	centi-	milli-

The **metre** is the **unit** of measurement, hence the decimal point is placed directly after this. If the unusual **hecta, deca** and **deci** are inserted it can be seen how they match the already established place values of the ordinary decimal system.

To change metres to centimetres, the centimetre becomes the unit and the point is moved accordingly and the spaces filled with 0s; e.g.:

kilo-	hecta-	deca-	metre	deci-	centi-	milli-
			5.			
			5	0	0.	

6   When working with directed numbers (e.g. −5) some children with directional confusion find number lines difficult. These numbers appear to be more easily understood when related to personal finance; e.g.:

$$-7 + (-5)$$

I owe £7.00 and I owe £5.00 so I owe £12 = −12

$$-3 + 4$$

I owe £3 and I am given £4 so I have £1.00 = 1

$$7 - (-5)$$

I have £7 and the debt of £5 is taken away, so I actually have a credit of £12.00 = 12

7   Mnemonics are as valuable in maths as they are for spelling.

(a) Many children have relied on **BODMAS** to see them through the appropriate sequence of steps in a problem that requires more than one process.

B = Brackets
O = Of
D = Divide
M = Multiply
A = Add
S = Subtract

(b) The dunce's hat is a well-known aid for **D**istance/**S**peed/**T**ime calculations.

$$\therefore\ D = S \times T$$

$$T = \frac{D}{S}$$

$$S = \frac{D}{T}$$

(c) Equations for the use of **S**in, **C**os and **T**an to find the angles and sides of a right-angled triangle can be remembered either by **SOHCAHTOA**

$$S = \frac{O}{H} \qquad C = \frac{A}{H} \qquad T = \frac{O}{A}$$

or **T**he **O**ld **A**merican **S**at **O**n **H**is **C**ar **A**nd **H**iccupped.

$$T = \frac{O}{A} \qquad S = \frac{O}{H} \qquad C = \frac{A}{H}$$

Conclusions

As with all aspects of teaching, the child himself may well come up with useful memory aids and strategies, but to achieve this he needs time to **talk** through his numeracy work.

It is now widely recognised that children should *understand* why they are dealing with figures in a particular way rather than mechanically carrying out a process. The logic of maths and preciseness of being right or wrong is very reassuring to some children. However, there are also those for whom maths is a complete enigma and they have a deep-seated conviction that they will never understand. Overcoming this particular hurdle by being taught in the way they learn brings about a marked improvement and even an enthusiasm for the subject.

Chapter 12

Study skills

Many mildly dyslexic children manage to cope at school with minimal or no help, perhaps falling short of their potential but managing an acceptable level of achievement. However, a number do find it a particular struggle when they reach the level of working for exams and when the quantity of work expected has greatly increased. They read and write a little more slowly than their fellows, or need to read everything a second time in order to extract the meaning. Time, or the lack of it, is a perpetual problem. Add to this any difficulty with self-organisation and the result may be a sudden deterioration in attainment, loss of confidence and feelings of despair about failing to reach adequate goals for their future careers.

All children benefit from study skills which should promote insight into how each one of them works most effectively, but dyslexic children need more guidance than others to develop these skills. While it is often recognised that teenagers need this support, it is an area of the curriculum that is just as valuable for older children in primary schools. It can easily be covered with whole groups or classes, and the constructive and useful discussions that evolve can be part of the spoken language component of the English curriculum.

Assessing needs

Children need to stop and think about their own situations in order to appreciate where exactly their difficulties lie. Is it only with spelling and punctuation or also with completing homework, planning and writing essays, note-taking, writing up notes, remembering information, using resources, revision or answering exam questions? Likewise, what are their strengths? Is it in diagrams, can they remember mnemonics, do they find it easier to remember the spoken or written part of any lesson? Making a list of their own strengths and weaknesses gives a base-line from which to start. Subsequent group discussions can be very encouraging as pupils pick up ideas from one another and find that several of them share certain difficulties.

Children should be encouraged to think how they can help themselves overcome short spans of concentration. Do they remember to look at the face of the teacher while he or she is speaking, or are they looking out of the window? Where do they sit in the class and is it a good position for them? Who sits next to them and is he or she a distraction? What positive steps are *they* taking to improve the situation?

Organising time

Older pupils should list the time they have available for homework and revision outside lessons. If possible, these times should be divided into units of approximately 40 minutes, as this is a good length for working before concentration levels begin to fall.

To avoid build-up of work and frantic last-minute panics, homework can then be allocated to specific times, spaced throughout the week. There should also be some time made available for *catching up* and reviewing work covered that week; this can well be done by spending 5 minutes looking back through their notes or exercise book as part of the daily subject homework assignment. As work is set, it can be written in against pre-planned times in a homework diary and then crossed out when completed. This should balance work evenly throughout the week and will prevent any of it being forgotten. Sticking to the plan, in itself, saves time as the decision of what to do has already been made.

Some children need guidance to work out a realistic plan. Time for relaxation and social events must be incorporated. It is useless to allocate work for 9.00 a.m. on a Sunday if lying-in on a Sunday is a habit, or on a Saturday afternoon if football matches are the order of the day. After a week, the plan can be reviewed and amended as problem areas may become apparent.

Projects and course work are difficult to plan for as the pupil may have very little idea how long the work may take him. As a general rule it is usually a bit longer than foreseen! It is imperative not to postpone the start of the project and to set a deadline just ahead of that given by the teacher. So often final *copying up* can take longer than expected, and a dyslexic student must leave more time than most for checking the completed work.

Keywords

Before making notes from any written text, or answering any question, pupils should learn to pick out the keywords. These should be underlined (once or twice) or highlighted, written in capitals or put in boxes; in other words, any way which will draw immediate attention. When taking notes from a textbook it can be helpful to use a clear plastic sheet and clip this over a page and then highlight the information wanted without actually marking the book.

Having found the keywords, the child will have the basis for making notes or answering the question. Correct interpretation of the question is very important in order to answer appropriately and give the different type of answer required; for example, **account for, describe, compare, differentiate, explain, evaluate, interpret, illustrate, define, justify, discuss, demonstrate.**

When reading texts or school-books, many children are unaware of how very important it is for them to look at chapter headings, diagrams, footnotes, first and last paragraphs. By looking at these *before they begin to read* the main text, they become tuned-in to the general gist and keywords which aid comprehension. In actual comprehension exercises it is good to read the question before the text for the same purpose of keying in. Teachers can still insist that the text is read twice before the questions are attempted.

If notes have to be written on a set topic they can become very muddled if there is too wide a choice of reference material. Dyslexic children, more than any others, need specific guidelines to know where to begin, how to make their points, and how to draw conclusions. It is better to suggest a couple of suitable books to use for the core plan. Then, if all has gone smoothly, they can look at other books and add details.

Planning essays

Younger children often find it hard to begin. Story Boards, which is writing a single sentence beneath a sequence of six pictures, is one well-tried method. Later they can learn to **build-a-story** from a simple three-word sentence; for example:

> The cat ran.
> **What sort of cat?**
> The young, thin black cat.
> **How did it run?**
> It ran quickly – like lightning.
> **Why did it run?**
> The dog chased it.
> **What sort of dog?**
> A big fierce shaggy dog.
> **Where did this happen?**
> **What was it like there?**
> **Why did the dog chase the cat?**
> **What happened in the end?**
> **How did the cat/dog feel?**

At the end of this discussion there is a complete story, including adjectives and adverbs, to expand the main idea. Or:

Introduction

<u>Who</u>	– cat – dog	slinky, black shaggy, large	<u>5 senses:</u>
			<u>sight</u>
<u>When</u>	– winter – afternoon	dark, shadows	
			<u>hearing</u>
<u>Where</u>	– garden, – town	quiet, traffic hum	
			<u>touch</u>

Core

<u>What</u>	– chase	yelps	
<u>How/Why</u>	– instinct	lightning	
			<u>smell</u>

Conclusion

| <u>Result</u> | – escape | panic
relief | <u>taste</u>
+
<u>emotions</u> |

The basic underlined lists on each side of the page can be used for any narrative or descriptive story. The idea that writing is making pictures out of words for the reader is helpful and, therefore, links between the senses and the scene and characters are essential.

Initially, the first step is to interpret the keywords in the title and draw up a rough plan of ideas. The essays must have an introduction, core and conclusion. In a factual or opinion type of essay the title often leads straight into the introduction, to be followed by main ideas or events. If these are jotted down in circular **web** form, sometimes known as **spider diagrams**, as they occur to the writer, they can then be linked by numbers or colour and discarded as appropriate. This usually avoids the lack of structure that could happen if the ideas were written in the order in which they had come to mind. It is useful to decide on the conclusion first of all – perhaps even the wording of the final sentence – in order to ensure that the train of thought all goes to that one end. The plan should not include sentences, but should be written in as few words as possible, and abbreviations are acceptable. It is useful to indicate proposed paragraphs by numbering.

Example of essay plan – factual or opinion type

'There are those who believe there should be a return of Capital Punishment. Discuss the main issues.'

KEY WORDS IN TITLE = Return, C.P., Discuss.

① **INTRO:** current terrorism/police etc. ∴ call for C.P.

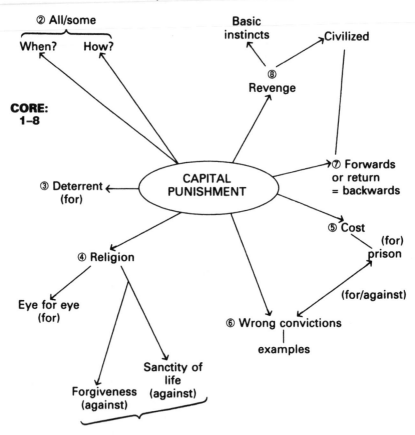

② All/some

When?   How?

Basic instincts   Civilized

⑧ Revenge

CORE: 1–8

③ Deterrent (for)

CAPITAL PUNISHMENT

→⑦ Forwards or return = backwards

④ Religion

⑤ Cost (for) prison

Eye for eye (for)

(for/against)

⑥ Wrong convictions

examples

Sanctity of life (against)

Forgiveness (against)

⑦ **CONCLUSIONS:**
Final sentence: Hence, a return to C.P. would seem to be a retrograde step in a civilized society.

Essay writing is a part of every pupil's requirements. Many are taught the principles in their English lessons but do not automatically apply these to other subjects. Many a school report mentions **poor essays, undeveloped ideas in essays,** and so on, but it is an area where some children need positive support and suggestions. Analysis of examples of a few good essays in the required subject can show how basic plans have been developed. To work from a good sample essay back to a plan, and then later to re-write the essay from this plan is helpful.

Planning course work

Time spent making a plan before launching into a project is time very well spent.

The title or questions should give the keywords as to what is important. From this a list can be made dividing the project into parts for how, and from where, the information is to be gathered. An introduction and conclusion will be required, and it is helpful to keep a list of books and other resources *as* they are being used. A list of diagrams or illustrations that will be of use should also be made. The analogy can be made of a cook gathering together the ingredients for a successful meal. It is a pity if a vital ingredient is found to be missing after the cooking has begun!

Junior children are becoming far more proficient at this type of planning with the requirements of the National Curriculum. For instance, in Science they are well used to setting out a list of the equipment they need, explaining step by step what was done and, finally, writing a conclusion. This format can give a good frame on which other subjects can be built too.

For pupils who find this difficult, it can be helpful to take a simple activity such as **making a cup of tea** and asking them to describe this in the same way. First, to list everything needed; second, to sequence each step correctly and simply. Much amusement can be gained by thinking literally and realising that we do *not* **boil a kettle.**

Note-taking

Notes need to be organised because their purpose is for later reference. Clearly set-out work with underlined headings is important. Sub-sections can be marked A. B. C.; (a) (b) (c); I, II, III; 1, 2, 3; (i) (ii) (iii). **Linear notes,** as these are called, with clear headings, make it easier for the pupil to find the information he wants later on. If the teacher gives headings and sub-section numbers when putting up notes for pupils to copy, or when dictating, the result is usually a clearer outline.

However, it is important to remember that those with a poor ability to retain the image of words will only be copying a few words, or even letters, at a time. Those without a difficulty in spelling can read a phrase or sentence, hold it in their minds and write it. In doing this they are generally also absorbing the sense of what they write. It is all too easy to take this for granted. If holding the image is difficult, and words have to be looked at carefully – sometimes two or three times because spelling is poor – the sense is often lost.

Likewise with dictated notes, some pupils are so occupied in hanging on to the words in order to write them, again perhaps having to try to recall spellings, that they, too, have very little sense of the meaning of what they have actually written down. Furthermore, the notes themselves deteriorate rapidly and will not be of great value at a later date (see Example A).

Example A

~~Lighting and power points~~

it is important that lighting is adduacuet for comfortball
and safe worki working weather it is light from
windows   or   lighting   Artyfishall light shanld
be   put   to in Sure that they are not sadows
over sink or working plats places Srip
Tighting , 1 Spot tight can be use for
spaces   they   Shaud be lots of pawer
point   at   a   convey ner Height for
bte efert id aplans use And changing
Plug is a newsanse and esetel
 bte dangers tranlling fleacs are dang
ers .

This example shows rapid deterioration in writing from the dictated Home Economics notes of a 16-year-old boy.

Many dyslexic pupils find they have better recall for diagrams and pictures than for words. Linear notes may not be as effective for them as web notes (spider diagrams) for essay planning, or mind maps. For mind maps the main topic is written in the centre of the page. As main themes are mentioned or thought of, a line is drawn from the circle and the theme word printed as for a sub-heading. As each theme is expanded, further lines branch out. Finally, with colours and numbers and possibly even with pictures, the points can be linked and sorted into a logical order for essays.

The greater the use of colour and sketches on the notes, the better they act as a memory aid for revision purposes. Indeed, a useful form of revision is to make a web from a set of linear notes and then refer to this for quick revision.

Example of linear notes (headings only)

Wall Street Crash (1929)

A *Causes*

1 Uneven distribution of wealth
2 Speculation
3 Protection tariffs
4 Over-production   (a) agriculture
                                       (b) industry
5 Hire purchase
6 Agricultural problems   (a) Johnson Act
                                       (b) cotton → synthetics
                                       (c) horse → mechanism
                                       (d) less demand
7 War debt and reparations
8 Unstable business structure (a) banks
                                       (b) monopolies
                                       (c) trusts and holding companies

B *Effects*

I *USA*

1 Economic disaster – chain reaction
2 Unemployment
3 Collapse of banks
4 Agricultural collapse
5 Breakdown of confidence
                                       (i) breadlines
                                       (ii) hobos
                                       (iii) hoovervilles
                                       (iv) sharecroppers

II *Europe*
   etc.

Some students find it beneficial to tape a talk or lecture and then work on the notes later when they are able to run and stop the tape at a speed that is suitable for them. Sometimes a friend's notes are helpful, but it is important that they choose to use some that are clear and correct. Those from a fellow dyslexic pupil could serve to add to the confusion!

Web notes made from preceding linear notes

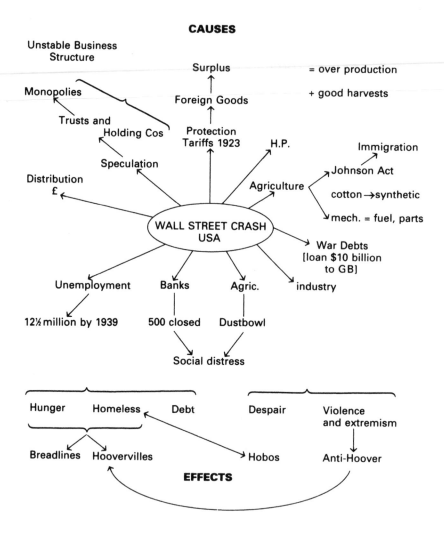

CAUSES

Unstable Business Structure

Monopolies

Trusts and Holding Cos

Surplus = over production
+ good harvests

Foreign Goods

Protection Tariffs 1923

Speculation

H.P.

Immigration

Johnson Act

Agriculture   cotton → synthetic

mech. = fuel, parts

Distribution £

WALL STREET CRASH USA

War Debts [loan $10 billion to GB]

Unemployment   Banks   Agric.   industry

12½ million by 1939   500 closed   Dustbowl

Social distress

Hunger   Homeless   Debt   Despair   Violence and extremism

Breadlines   Hoovervilles   Hobos   Anti-Hoover

EFFECTS

Abbreviations

If notes are dictated or to be copied, it is helpful for the pupils to be familiar with abbreviations:

∴ ∵ i.e. e.g. etc. N.B.

Then particular subjects may have particular abbreviations:

Parl.   =   Parliament
Govt.   =   Government
✕   =   Battle, etc.

Once a web is completed, each area should then be explained to someone else. This not only aids the memory, but reveals any misunderstanding or errors. By speaking aloud about the notes taken, this becomes a truly multisensory strategy.

The Mind Map Book by Tony Buzan has an excellent section on webs and his books are written with dyslexic people in mind so his strategies for note-taking are well worth putting into practice.

Reading

We use different reading techniques for different purposes.

1   *Light reading* for pleasure has no time limits and it is not necessary to recall everything that has been read.
2   *Skimming* is a process of just looking at selected parts, perhaps chapter headings, initial paragraphs, diagrams.
3   *Scanning* is searching through a piece of text looking for particular facts or information.
4   *Critical reading* requires full comprehension and analysis of what has been read. Facts, opinions, inferences have to be detected and understood.

Before embarking on critical reading, students should establish the habit of skimming first, and decide the purpose and direction they are following. Is it a series of events, connected ideas or contradictory opinions? What questions can they formulate in their minds that need answering? If necessary, note these down even if only in the form of Who? When? Where? What? Why? How? Jot down the keyword answers to these questions, and there is the basis for a set of notes. These keywords are an aid to recalling the main points which then can be re-expanded into essays.

Some students are quite overwhelmed by the library, and do not know how or where to begin in order to find relevant subject information. Practical exercises should be done in finding certain books, and then in using the index and contents pages.

Planning and checking work

Some students with a specific learning difficulty are allowed extra time in external exams. This time must be used constructively, and practice should be given in how it should be used. A rough mind map or web diagram is a good starting point. It requires a considerable amount of practice to convince students that time spent *planning before writing* an answer is generally time extremely well spent. It can be difficult to persuade children that in further education a third of the examination time is recommended for planning. If an initial plan has been made, each point and detail can be marked off as it is included.

There should always be time to check work after completing it. Course work and projects are often better checked the following day with a fresh mind. Ideally, each sentence should be read, from capital letter to full stop. This acts as a check for sense, sentence structure and punctuation.

Sentence construction should be kept simple. Complicated sub-clauses often lead to a change of tense in mid-sentence or two or three sub-clauses strung together without a main clause, as the pupil loses track of the subject. Children need to know where their own particular weaknesses lie and learn to check these areas with extra care. For instance, if punctuation is a weakness, the pupil has to learn that it is essential for him always to go back after writing the essay and check specifically for that. Reading their own work aloud often enables pupils to appreciate better how confused it may have become.

Example B

There is a person call Rowland Hill in the 19th Century who thaught it is a good a idea to put stamps on to letters. He talked to the Goverment, On the stamps Queen victoria is on it, they decided to do this because no fixed rate and it is not reliable and it is exspensive.

A useful rule of thumb is:

- think clearly what you are trying to say;
- state it simply;
- re-read for content;
- if time allows, check again for spelling.

The spelling may need to be checked separately. Again, older children should be alerted to the type of mistakes they tend to make and be advised to look for these specifically. Some find it useful to use the proof-reading technique of starting at the end and looking at each word working along each line from right to left. This means that each word is **looked at** rather than the brain taking over and the pupils **reading** what they meant to write and therefore not recognising the errors.

A good idea is to skim the text **forwards** for punctuation and meaning, but **backwards** for spelling because the emphasis will be to review each individual word out of context and thus be more critical about its structure and accuracy.

Revision

Many children assume that revision is adequate if they read through all their notes. This often serves to trigger the memory, and children feel that they remember and know a particular topic. However, when faced with an exam question that does not have the same **key** or **trigger** words, they suddenly find that they have forgotten large chunks, and consequently achieve low marks.

An explanation of the purpose of multisensory teaching, and how we learn and remember through *seeing, hearing, saying* and *writing*, can bring home the need for varied techniques.

Strategies

Any one of the following may be appropriate:

1   Read information aloud. Some pupils have said that later in an exam they can hear their own voice.
2   Recording information and playing it back, which can be done at odd times throughout the day.
3   Tapes of set English books (see Chapter 6, Reading).
4   Writing keywords and, later, trying to give as much information on each word as possible.
5   File cards of webs, flow diagrams, diagrams and formulae and key facts.

6   Use of colour.
7   Mnemonics, rhymes, pictures.

Ideally, information from a lesson needs to be brought back to mind later that same day. It may be helpful to run through the timetable at the end of the day and think of a positive fact learnt in each lesson. Another look at these facts the next day, and a further look a week later, will do much to ease the load of revision for exams. There is *not one right way* to revise for everybody, and a discussion of what each person finds easiest can emphasise the need for individual strategies.

Concentration spans may be limited and levels tend to fall, so it is far better for pupils to set themselves a programme of revision that gives them short breaks. Concentrated work of, say, 30 or 40 minutes, a review of this work for 5 minutes, a break of 10 minutes and a further review of that same work for 5 more minutes can be very effective. A longer break may be necessary before tackling a different topic. Other reading and watching television should be avoided during these 10-minute breaks.

Exams

It is now recognised by the various Education Departments that some pupils require appropriate provision to be made for them in external examinations. This may take the form of extra time, spelling errors not penalised, a scribe and so on. However, the school must make this request well before the exam takes place, and should be aware of how this is done by checking with the appropriate Examination Board where they will get advice. Universities and colleges of further education may also take account of specific needs. In the independent sector, the Common Entrance Board also allows extra time to be granted if the senior school is agreeable.

Working to time during exams is often particularly difficult for dyslexic students, and it is vital that they should have adequate practice in answering exam questions within a given period.

The work on planning and webs previously mentioned should stand them in good stead. They should realise that, unless stated, the questions can be done in any order, as long as these are clearly labelled. It often helps people to relax and gives them more confidence if they can start the exam with the questions that they know best. However, they should learn that over-running the time on one question can bring serious problems if some of the paper is then incomplete, particularly as the marks will not be distributed accordingly. If they do not have time to do the final question they may lose as much as twenty marks which cannot possibly be regained by the extra time spent on earlier questions.

Familiarity with actual sample exam papers is important. From these, children will learn to read carefully the rubric telling them how many questions must be answered in any section, what marks are allocated, and how much time they can afford to spend on each question. This familiarity can give them added confidence before they begin. Noting or underlining keywords on the question paper itself should also help them to stay *on track*.

Conclusions

Most teachers these days incorporate some strategies for study skills into the teaching of their particular subject. However, group or individual discussion on specific points is generally necessary. Certainly, constant nagging about lack of organisation without some constructive recommendations and help only serves to lower morale and erode confidence. Many children need on-going help and guidance to find out how best to organise both themselves and their work.

Chapter 13

Classroom management

Although the emphasis in this book is on looking at, and dealing with, the needs of the individual child, it is appreciated how difficult this may seem to a busy class teacher.

The way in which the teacher manages a class depends on a number of factors; for instance, the ages of pupils, size of class, support available. Vertical streaming, open-plan layout or ESL (English as a second language) pupils all add complications to the equation. However, there are some general points to consider, as there will almost certainly be at least one child encountering specific learning difficulties to some degree in every class.

When special needs help is available

If a child's difficulties are significant and the resources are there, the child should be receiving specific help. In this case there should be close liaison between the specialist teacher and the class teacher. Unfortunately, in practice, there is often insufficient time for communication. Conscientious teachers are often upset by the failure of a child to progress along with his peers and may become a little defensive, feeling that suggestions being made are, in fact, criticisms of their methods. This is where a real understanding of the nature of the difficulty is so important. Class teachers should be aware that dyslexic children need constant revision and that there will be *bad days* when everything that seemed to have been learnt the previous week has suddenly evaporated. Acceptance of this situation can do much to relieve the pressure felt by both teacher and pupil.

In many cases, extra help is provided within the classroom. This is generally of a supportive nature and designed to enable a child to cope with a particular topic or piece of work at that time. Although it is desirable to keep a child with his peers, such help may not always be in his best interest. Withdrawal from class and individual assessment of his specific needs should help him to develop the strategies to cope better with the whole curriculum. This, in the end, will be of greater benefit to him. It is important to look at the long-term interests of the child rather than the success or failures he has with individual pieces of work. The special needs teacher should also be aware of the difficulties imposed on the class teacher, who may be feeling that the one child who cannot afford to miss any explanation is not there at the time it is given.

Withdrawal need not be a stigma; so much depends on how the class teacher handles it; digs by classmates can be countered by reminding them of, for instance, his good artwork. The retort that he is studying linguistics will soon silence rude remarks! Children know from where the appropriate help is coming (both within class and outside it) and are always pleased to have it. However, it may be necessary for the class teacher to make allowances for the child who has put in sustained effort during the special help time. He may not be ready for another burst of activity. He may need time to collect his thoughts and his belongings together and sort out what he is meant to be doing when he rejoins the class; this he needs to be able to do with confidence, although things may have moved on quickly in his absence.

Communication

A full discussion of the nature of the difficulty at a level appropriate to the child's age and understanding often produces a very positive reaction from the child, who may have been worrying about his failures and of appearing to be stupid (see Chapter 1, Dyslexia, page 1). If dyslexia is the cause, in our experience it is extremely rare for a child to then sit back and use it as an excuse for not working hard. If he is confident that the teacher is aware of the nature of his difficulties and is helping him to overcome them, he remains well motivated. He needs realistic help and hope – a light at the end of the tunnel.

Some children find it hard to open up to their class teacher about the difficulties they may be experiencing, as so often such discussions are overheard or interrupted by their classmates. Class teachers should not, therefore, be surprised or feel they have failed if another teacher mentions a problem of which they have been unaware. The important factor is that communication is kept open at all times between all teachers, the child and parents.

The headteacher of one junior school issues each child with a notebook in which parents can write any worry they may have. Every morning, class teachers quickly check each book and pass on to the headteacher the few requests by parents to discuss a problem. The headteacher will be on the phone to them by 10 a.m. In this way any difficulties are aired and discussed in the early stages and well before a communication problem has arisen.

Parents are often apprehensive about approaching their child's class teacher to discuss any concern they may feel for fear of being thought to be a *fussy parent*. This worry may be increased because of their own dyslexic problems and feelings of guilt that it is through them that their child is suffering. Some parents are so upset that they just cannot accept that their child has these difficulties. They may put down their own inadequacy to being badly taught which, of course, is probably true, in that they will not have been taught in the way that was appropriate for them. If they pluck up the courage to approach a teacher and are told **not to worry, it will come in time**, they will be even more anxious not to approach the teacher a second time. Their child's inability to learn may, by then, have been put down to their own anxiety. A situation then builds up where parental anxiety may turn to aggression. In any situation where there is a lack of understanding, giving rise to feelings of guilt and/or inadequacy, there will be a tendency to criticise. This can make matters worse, with parents blaming the school and vice versa.

If it is hard for some parents to accept that their child has a learning problem, literature to back up the teacher's comments may be helpful. It is often a relief to talk to other parents in a similar situation, perhaps by joining the local Dyslexia Association (the address and telephone number can be obtained from the British Dyslexia Association, see page 194) or their national SPELD. They will then be supported by others and put in touch with people who can advise them.

The class teacher also has an important role in liaising with other teachers, particularly when subjects are separately taught. Dyslexia is not only a literacy problem; difficulties with sequencing and orientation, listening and following instructions need to be understood by those teaching music, PE, games and swimming and so on, in addition to the more academic areas of the curriculum – for the teacher's own sanity as well as the pupil's!

Classroom arrangements

Where the child sits in the class is important. If he has a very poor concentration span or is inclined to dream, he needs to be near the teacher so that his attention can be regained discreetly if necessary. However, if the teacher is at a desk where many children bring work or wordbooks, concentration may be very difficult. He is constantly aware of, and disturbed by, the comings and goings and he may be better further away, but supported by a well-motivated and sympathetic classmate or Learning Support Assistant.

Flexibility in seating for primary children is important. It may be tempting to group children with difficulties on to one table. Although this is at times useful, particularly perhaps for sharing maths equipment, it is unfortunate if a group of children consider themselves **the slow ones** and are denied the positive influence from peers.

For some children it is important to sit in the centre of the classroom and face the board or OHP screen for any work that involves copying. Poor lighting may be creating an additional problem. Even the minimal annoyance of a reflecting board or dazzling screen can be the final straw for a child who is already struggling. Copying from a book or notes beside him may be easier if it can be arranged. A useful arrangement may be to borrow the book of a child whose notes are always clear.

Simple things matter: good organisation of equipment so that *he* knows where to find things, sufficient space to work, some quiet times in the day when he can focus his thoughts.

Concentration

Not all children, when asked, understand what concentration means, so the remark that it must be improved will have little effect.

If children *must learn to concentrate*, they *need to be taught*. One teacher used to read a short passage from a newspaper to a class and then ask ten factual questions on it. Usually the children had been fiddling with pencils, daydreaming and so on and failed to get many answers correct. The teacher would then talk to them about concentration and compare it with a television programme when the camera homes in on, for example, an animal, gradually shutting out peripheral detail until the animal's face alone is featured. The children then crossed their arms (no fiddling!) and thought only about the newspaper passage, which she re-read. This time there was a vast improvement in their answers. In this way they were able to realise the advantage of concentrating on the matter in hand. Card games, such as Matching Pairs, Kim's Game and other memory games all help concentration and may be played with the family at home.

However, there is a recognised limit of concentration when listening, a fact to be remembered especially when a subject teacher has a double lesson. A child may be able to concentrate for hours on an activity like Lego, which has an absorbing interest for him, but his concentration on a subject or skill that he finds difficult may be very limited. Everyone has this difficulty.

Copying

Teachers often fail to have sympathy with spelling errors when the word **merely had to be copied** to be correct. It should be remembered that some children experience difficulty with copying, especially from the board. Consequently, they are not, in fact, taking in any of the information in front of them. If the teacher has not carefully gone through and explained these notes first, pupils will refer to them for homework or, when older, as revision for exams, and may look at the notes as though they are full of new information that they have never before seen. If the teacher can supply ready-made notes and pupils learn to highlight key points, it may be a more effective use of their time. Sometimes a copy of another pupil's notes will be clearer for revision purposes. These need to be carefully chosen and, of course, be copied with the approval of the friend.

One of the greatest problems for dyslexic children can be completing assignments in a given time. Often their copying or listening skills are poor, and they are frantically trying to keep up before material is erased from the board or the teacher moves on to the next point. A class teacher can help improve the speed of copying for some children by underlining or marking every second line of the text on the board in a different colour.

Dictated notes

Dictated notes may fail to serve a useful purpose if they are not clear, the handwriting is poor and the spelling peculiar. Once again, many dyslexic children, both in junior and secondary schools, do not absorb any of the content as they are so busy dealing with the actual process of holding the words in their memories, spelling accurately and writing legibly. They do better if they merely listen to the dictation, perhaps write down occasional keywords and then are given the full notes afterwards. Highlighting the notes with colour, using their keywords, is then a useful form of revision.

Personal organisation

(See Chapter 12, Study skills.) Poor organisational skills are often present and need to be tackled from the beginning. Developing the child's own self-reliance and responsibilities is important and this should start early on in school life. For instance, instead of the parents packing the games clothes on a Tuesday and recorder on a Thursday, the child should learn to have a daily routine. If need be, he should ask or check which day it is, decide what is needed at school the next day (perhaps by referring to a chart or timetable kept in his bedroom), find it, put it in the school bag and check that the homework, pencils and so on are all there too. He may have to refer to a checklist each evening. Perhaps he needs to learn to carry a basic **survival kit** consisting of pen, pencil, ruler, rubber, wordbook, dictionary, table square and so on. A few children need to keep one kit at home and one at school.

In the same way, as soon as he is able, he should be encouraged to be really systematic about his work, and the younger this starts the better.

Headings and dates are important and should be there on every piece of work, and regular checks should be made by the teacher that all work is being kept in an orderly fashion, using folders, dividers and so forth. Many of these children are not being lazy or careless, but are genuinely hampered by extremely poor organisational skills; consequently, *they need positive support rather than constant nagging criticism* for loss of work, late assignments or homework not handed in. This disorganisation is one of the most irritating features for any parent or teacher to have to deal with. Older students benefit from a tutor who regularly checks that their files and notes are in reasonable order.

The sequencing of ideas, handwriting and spelling may all require extra thought and effort. Consequently, dyslexic children will not be as quick as those who do not have to concentrate on all three at once. Furthermore, as a pupil progresses he should be learning to check through and attempt some corrections of his work. It is absolutely imperative that he has the time to plan initially, and check at the end, and he needs to be given specific time within class to do this. A warning could be given that he must stop writing and check his work 5 minutes before the end of the lesson.

Homework

Homework is another problem area. By the end of the day a dyslexic child is generally more tired than his peers because everything requires more thought, takes longer and does not come easily. When tired, his difficulties – as with all of us – are more apparent, and he may make even more errors. The amount and type of homework should, therefore, be carefully considered. Different schools introduce homework at different ages. Even in primary schools where homework is not expected, a child may regularly be asked to catch up on the day's work. In the independent sector, homework may be expected from a very early age. Essays, creative written work and comprehension exercises may all be too much for a dyslexic child at this stage of the day. With the agreement of the class teacher, parents are often happy to write or type a child's oral account. Real value comes from exercises that provide reinforcement or revision and give an opportunity for reflective thought on work already covered that day. Many of these children spend far longer than the allocated time because they do not wish to present less than their peers and be shown up in class, or because a teacher decides that an exercise must be completed. It is not unknown for a conscientious teenager to write corrected essays long into the night and get up early to finish other assignments. Inevitably, there is a build-up of tiredness and exhaustion affecting all aspects of their lives.

Similarly, it is unhelpful for pupils to gain the habit of spending an hour on a question that may only be allocated half that time in an exam. It is better to work for the half hour and learn how to make the most use of that time. A parent's note may be the first indication that class and subject teachers have of excessive time being spent on homework.

When allocating homework and exercises that may be a little different or less demanding, it is important to exercise tact. Self-esteem is rapidly undermined if a teacher is underlining the differences between those with difficulties and their peers. Expectations should be realistic and the pupil should then meet them, and doubtless along with others there will be times when the teacher is quite correct that *not enough effort has been made*. However, it should always be remembered that far more effort is needed for them to achieve the same as their peers.

When homework is set it is important to check that children correctly write down *exactly* what is required. So often they write a shorthand version and then memory fails them at home; or they write down the wrong exercise or page number. It is a good idea for them to have the telephone numbers of a couple of friends so that if there is any last-minute doubt they can ring up and check rather than worry or spend time doing the wrong work.

Project work

Topic work always requires preparation by the teacher. It is useful to build up a store of plastic envelopes, colour-coded for content. Some envelopes should hold cards on which there are four or five pictures with a single word for each picture. Others should have descriptive words, and others action words linked to the topic. Basic language structure is provided in this way, which the child can then copy. Another envelope would have useful generalities; for example, **there were, it was, it is, a/the/an** and so on.

Take, for instance, the topic **Flight**

pictures such as	=	**bird, balloon, plane, feather**
adjectives	=	**light, heavy**
action	=	**float, flap** or **fly, flies, flew**

This teaches the idea of building up sentences from keywords, which in due course will benefit their writing.

Corrections

Work corrected by a teacher should be returned as soon as possible so that it is still fresh in the child's mind. Ideally, corrections should be done with the children. In junior schools this is the province of the class teacher, but in secondary schools and colleges this may have to come within the tutor's orbit. It is not realistic to expect all the spelling errors to be corrected, but there is a more lasting and positive effect if only one point – such as double letters or full stops – is picked out. Sentence construction for some is as difficult as spelling because they have no natural feel for syntax. Credit should be given for content wherever appropriate. If a child knows all the capital cities for a geography test, does he really deserve 2/10 because he has made spelling errors? So many children are really hurt by the comments at the end of their work. Sometimes, they are fortunate in having difficulty in deciphering the teacher's handwriting as this may save their feelings!

Example

I₅ 1890 – 1918 Guns were breech loading and Quick firing types. They were used in the Boer war and the first world wa During the first world war guns improved. Machine guns were invented and so were armoured monsters armed with two six pounders. These monsters were called Tanks.

(p=)   Tor much of a attempt. what did you on this?

Apart from written comments, many of us looking back over the years can remember teachers' hurtful remarks about our efforts when we were in vulnerable situations. These comments may have been light-hearted on the part of the teacher at the time, but can still be a painful memory many years later. It should be remembered that the dyslexic child does not leave all his difficulties behind as he leaves the classroom. Punishments that may be considered in order for some, such as writing lines and essays, are doubly onerous and therefore unsuitable for a child who finds writing difficult. Likewise, being kept in at break to catch up is often counter-productive. He needs the chance to let off steam and come back to the classroom a little refreshed.

Liaising with subject teachers

Children with moderate difficulties often slip through the net. As most schools allocate a class teacher or tutor to oversee each child's pastoral needs, part of their brief could be to liaise with colleagues to smooth the way. Subject teachers can help by providing vocabulary – lists of words relevant to their subject – which can be kept at the back of a file or notebook as a quick reference point for checking spellings. Eileen Stirling's **Check List** is a useful aid for older children. Younger children can have an equivalent list of irregular words that they find particularly difficult; these can be written on a card that they can refer to at any time.

Foreign languages, particularly French, often prove exceptionally difficult because the dyslexic pupil is unable to use the ground rules of sound–letter association that he may have established to help his English, such as **we/oui**. Visually, some of the letter strings in the two languages are also quite different – for example, **deux, suis, cinq** – and there are added complications of accents. French is often taught from a topic vocabulary base, rather than through the whole grammatical structure of the language which may be what these children find easier. Grammar *is* important because it is language structure. Without mutually recognisable structure which is understood, communication becomes impossible or at best unreliable. Generally German is found to be more regular, and Spanish possibly easiest. After English, Spanish is the most widely spoken language, but unfortunately is not always available as a choice of second language.

Subject textbooks often prove to have a reading age above that of the child. It should be remembered that a reading age is based on general vocabulary. Class teachers are no doubt aware that a science textbook, for instance, may prove very much harder to read than a reading test as the words used are unfamiliar.

Learning Support Teachers or SENCOs in large schools may have difficulties in managing to speak to all the teachers about any one child. If, however, at intervals there can be in-service training to explain the nature of these difficulties and the terminology used, it is then possible on a termly basis (because memories are short!) to circulate a list of children requiring support, with a brief comment highlighting their particular needs. This list should include those needing help in certain areas, even if they are not considered weak enough to have full support from the Special Needs Department.

Dictionaries

It is never too soon for a child to learn to use a dictionary. Different dictionaries suit different children. For example, the *ACE Spelling Dictionary* and the *Oxford Mini Dictionary of Spelling and Word Division* are two that have proved especially good for children with spelling problems. Others find a small dictionary of synonyms and antonyms worthwhile. For instance, if in doubt about the spelling of **enormous** the child looks up **big** and will find not only **enormous** but other appropriate words as well – thus extending vocabulary at the same time. Children with weak speech and language processing find sentence dictionaries particularly helpful as the words are used in context. Some dictionaries include word derivations which are of particular value to older children. Also of value is *Roget's Thesaurus*, and there are simpler versions of thesauruses for young children.

Different types of dictionaries are needed for different purposes – some for spelling, some for word use and some for derivations – and children need to be taught how to use them (see Chapter 9, Sequencing). Young children can begin by cutting out pictures and making a very simple dictionary to develop an awareness of initial sounds.

Computers

Computers, word-processors and spell-checks are now commonplace in classrooms and can be of great benefit to children of all ages. It is such a fast-developing field that specific recommendations of equipment and software soon become dated, but the British Dyslexia Association (see Addresses, page 194) has a computer committee and publishes a comprehensive list of programs that may be of particular help.

A dyslexic pupil may have particular strengths with the visual–spatial skills required to manipulate computer graphics and data. Appropriate use of computers can do much to compensate for areas of weakness in literacy skills.

Re-motivation of a child who has become a reluctant learner is a frequent bonus achieved with the use of a computer. A machine has the advantage of being non-judgemental and ever-patient! Programs may be tailored to an individual's needs for levels of difficulty, speed and/or repetition and the final result is generally more attractive, especially for a child with handwriting problems. Many programs, which record all the attempts and errors made during an exercise, can be set by a busy teacher, enabling her, at a more convenient time, to note these and to evaluate and adjust her teaching accordingly.

Computers can be used to run on structured remedial practice, but huge benefits can be obtained with the use of word-processing. The facility to file, edit and revise text, perhaps manipulating sentence or paragraph order, as well as to run a spell-check, can be invaluable. However, the subsequent filing and organisation of print-outs may require guidance and attention from the teacher.

To maximise efficient use of such technology the child must be given the opportunity to learn and practise fluency on the keyboard. Touch typing is the ideal but the chances of access to tuition in this are very limited, particularly in primary schools. However, time to learn to become proficient is essential. A word-processor given to help with exams is of limited use to someone having to search for the letters! Keyboard fluency also enables the dyslexic child to take a full part in accessing CD Roms and other aspects of the curriculum on an equal footing with his peers. In using a computer with voice feedback, it should be remembered that speaking and writing are two different forms of communication and both need to be specifically taught and learnt.

Care should be taken in the choice of computer games and activities. Some of these require a fairly advanced level of reading. Many spelling programs do not take into account the particular requirements of each dyslexic child. For instance, visual letter clusters occur such as **rough, through, although** and **thorough,** without the phonic back-up which might be necessary. Likewise, in the choice of a spell-check, some are visually based and some have a phonic element; for example, **diside** entered on one with a visual base will produce **divide** but not **decide.** Yet again, how the individual functions is important when choosing equipment.

Conclusions

The other chapters in this book explain specific problems and outline help in different areas, but a sympathetic and positive general approach can do so much to alleviate a child's anxieties and remove unnecessary pressures. Credit for effort as well as achievement are both essential. *Ideally, every lesson should begin with an outline of what is going to be taught and end with a résumé of what has been taught.* Where possible, the connecting links could be pointed out between this work or topic and what has already been covered. In this way information is more likely to go from short-term to long-term memory. This practice is of value to all the children in the class.

It must not be assumed that every child can successfully absorb information from a teacher in the same way. Especially in senior schools, the subject being taught is given priority, possibly overlooking this fact. It is accepted that we all have different abilities, *but it is also true that we all have different ways of learning.* The chosen method of presentation may seem ideal from the teacher's viewpoint, but if some children do not learn from the way the teacher is presenting the information, they will fail and therefore eventually lose interest in the subject.

Some children find it easier to absorb information auditorily without the distraction of writing notes. Others will take it in better through being able to visualise the written word, and notes are therefore a useful channel;

yet others will appreciate the back-up of diagrams and colour emphasis because they visualise pictorially.

Supplying all these methods of presentation may seem to be an impossible task. *But one must teach in different ways in order to teach the whole class.* If teachers will bear this in mind when planning their lessons, they can include strategies which apply these methods to each topic. Their effort will be repaid in the long run by improved performance, more interest and better relationships with the children.

Those who are strong auditorily should have the opportunity to look at a visualiser's notes, and diagrams may also be devised to share with the rest of the class. All this sharing can take place during time put aside at the end of the lesson for reinforcement – or even later if children become enthusiastic about different ways of presentation.

It is interesting, and often revealing, to ask pupils to write down what they, in particular, find helpful or unhelpful at school. Here are a few unsolicited comments taken from junior and secondary pupils:

UNHELPFUL

In certain lessons teachers seem to spend more time explaining why someone shouldn't do something like wasting time and than the person was in the first place.

1. notes because you get a few unmeaningfull words.

Sometime it is hard copying off the board if there is many words.

Teacher not fully answering your questions

I might have to stop to spell a word and miss the next sentence.

2. dictation because of spelling mistakes and they quickly read through and you get lost.

1 if there is to much riting on a black bord at one time you can lose your place.

reading around the class because some people find it hard to read and they find it difficult and then you don't I understand

question that are long worded Some teachers writing is ~~easy~~ not easy to read

Teachers ignoring you

reading out aloud

teacher expect notes to be taken down quickly and word often become illegible. short examinations.

Complaining at you when your not really at fought

Complaining at you when your not really at fought

Abbreviation are used to often and are difficult to understand.

I can inot work if they shout at me.

HELPFUL

Going through things Before Because it is easyer spocken then when it is writen.

I would like to be on my own with the teacher Just an hour a day.

The teacher should . be kind and understanding so they will be friends with the teachers.

Giving you lots of practise on certain things so that you get it stuck in your mind.

It is helpful that teachers exeplaned that subject that pupil are doing.

REVISION   for revision   It would help
to have   it pre recorded on tape especially
for GCSE exams. rather than Just reading
through our notes.

Writing things up on
the board and explaining
it.

Children should not be rushed when doing
work, they should take there time because
if they are rushed then they will get
things wrong and endid up getting shouted
at and we would all end up know where.

1. If a child gets something wrong they shouldn't
be shouted at, they should be able to talk
to the teacher and be able to have it more
explained

It has helped me to have a quiyot class.

Going through things
with you, and making
sure you understand
it.

Thinking.   If we do projects then I think that
we Should spend 1 lesson Just thinking about
rather than Just rushing in and Starting it then
finding out that we made a mistake and
have to Start again.

Putting certain things
in a different way
to make it easier.

(29) Extre time to check

notc copying

I think that notes should be ready done
so that we don't have to copy notes down us
we often don't have enough time so we
have to rush it and then we can't read it.
But if it was on ready made notes we could read
them and Take them in.

Chapter 14

Summary

Dyslexia has been a matter of contention over the years, almost like a religion, with those who believe and those who do not. Often, it takes a personal situation for a disbeliever suddenly to realise what it is all about. If it is not understood, a teacher's frustration may lead to criticism of a child, and parental anxiety may turn to aggression. Parents tend to blame the school and the school may blame the parents, and the child is the victim in the centre. Before this situation develops, a meeting needs to be arranged between teacher and parents. First of all, the following should be clarified:

- Is the child's sight normal? Not only is it important to check for long- or short-sightedness, but also for the ability to focus at near range for reading and the ability to focus on the board and tracking along a line of print.
- Is the child's hearing normal? May hearing be intermittent due to catarrh or glue ear?

Then a discussion should include a checklist as follows:

1 Is the child understanding what is said? Has he ever had speech therapy?
2 Has the child adequate vocabulary to express himself?
3 Is the child's reading adequate for his intellectual needs and class requirements?
4 Is the child's spelling bizarre or an inadequate attempt at applying phonics?
5 Does he have difficulty sequencing alphabet, days, months, multiplication tables – assuming these have been taught?
6 Does he have spatial problems (right and left, telling the time, getting from A to B, directional confusions in maths)?
7 Is he very disorganised (more than the others), forgetful, invariably in the wrong place, always getting lost, and usually late?

8 Does he look wan and worried, switched off, and appear not to be thriving?

9 Is he lagging behind the class, unable to keep up?

10 Is there a history of such difficulties in the family?

Also of importance, but to be mentioned tactfully:

- Are there problems at home which may be worrying him?
- Does he get on with all his teachers?

Although there may be problems at home and a child may not get on with his teacher, most children are resilient enough for these situations not to be the primary cause of an educational problem. Awareness of either situation should not preclude consideration of a specific learning difficulty. Nevertheless, the lack of self-confidence, which most dyslexic children experience, needs to be taken into account and to counteract this, it is important for them to enjoy something that they are good at.

The next step may be a discussion with the Head of Special Needs (SENCO) and then an appointment with an educational psychologist. Many a child has found that an assessment and the resulting label of dyslexia have been an enormous relief. He then knows that he is not stupid or lazy and that there is a reason for his academic failure, and this is reassuring. Determination to get on top of the problem replaces previous bewilderment.

Many mildly dyslexic children, and even those who are moderately so, may not have such an assessment, but can find great reassurance from an explanation of dyslexia by an understanding teacher. Unfortunately, some of these dyslexic children slip through the net unrecognised and without help. Remarks on their school reports, such as **Could do better, Must concentrate, Essay writing poor, Must try harder, Must improve your spelling,** are all too frequent and should alert the teacher to investigate further (see English report on page 186).

On the other hand, the positive approach used on many school Statements of Achievement, while commendable in one way, can lead to a false sense of security. Underlying problems are then glossed over only to become apparent later when the pupil is faced with GCSE exams.

Luke, aged 12 years, with a high average IQ, wrote the following for a dictation:

> One day two small boys went camping down by the river. They were geuts begine to put up thege tent went sodinle it started to ran.

His Statement of Achievement gave the impression that there was no particular problem and that he merely needed to be more consistent with his proof-reading.

ENGLISH

Form   L4

Name   R. ☐

Richard makes great professions of diligence, but has not mustered the discipline to overcome personal disorganization and increasingly messy handwriting. His contribution to class discussion is excellent but his written work, whilst interesting, often indicates a lack of careful consideration of ideas.

☐

In order to be able to teach, as far as possible, according to each child's educational needs, it is essential to see him or her as a whole person, complete with individual learning strengths and weaknesses. In order to get the fullest possible picture, especially of those with specific learning difficulties, co-operation from, and discussion with, other professionals is important. There would be more understanding of their work and barriers would be broken down if these professional people were invited more often to talk to staff at schools.

It is very important to get a balanced viewpoint, because otherwise one professional person may draw conclusions from his or her own training alone. For example, a psychologist is trained to look at psychological aspects, and so a child's reading difficulties may be put down to family problems rather than lack of ability to visualise words and make the phonological links. The same misunderstanding may occur with children whose first language is not English; if they have reading and spelling problems in both their first language and English, it is as well to consider dyslexia as a possible cause. An eminent paediatrician, Dr White Franklin, who became very much involved with the controversy surrounding dyslexia in the 1960s and 1970s, used to say that in any situation regarding a child, various points of view would be put forward. For instance, supposing that a small child is playing with building bricks, the neurologist may be considering his hand–eye coordination; the artist would be interested in his choice of colours; an architect might be interested in the type of construction; a speech and language therapist would be listening to his articulation and speech processes as he played; the teacher may be interested in his development by that age; and the parent might be looking at the expression on his face. Consequently, discussion among these different professionals would produce the most cohesive picture of that individual child. A similar situation applies to parents, class teachers and other professionals.

Both parents and teachers need to be wary of predicting the outcome of a child's education. There is an unknown quantity – an unrecognisable dimension – that makes forecasting unreliable. Confidence can develop and learning strategies may *come together*. With an increasing determination to succeed the child wins through, often in his own untraditional, individual way. This cannot be assessed in tests. One child was written off by his headmaster with **He'll never do very much, poor boy!** and ended up with an upper second degree in Economics and later became a chartered accountant. Another boy with a low average IQ on the Wechsler Intelligence Scale for Children gained a degree in Ceramics and a year or two later a further degree, with honours, in Sculpture. Success tends to breed success. Once on the way, progress may become rapid. An understanding attitude on the part of the teachers – and the right approach to tuition – can very quickly change a negative situation and enable a child to thrive. Now that dyslexia is becoming much more recognised, there are many more of these success stories.

Throughout their school careers, many dyslexic children are continually faced with failure and criticism of their work. Teachers, trying to be helpful, point out the need for them to raise their standards. Loss of confidence often follows, and this can be one of the most damaging results of dyslexia. Learning to deal with failure, and in some instances criticism, may, of course, be a valuable lesson for life – *provided that the failure and criticism do not crush them*. Parental support and faith in their child, without undue pressure, is important. Humour plays a vital role. Learning to laugh at one's mistakes is helpful at any time in life.

Positive attitudes, if acquired by dyslexic children, stand them in good stead later. Some older pupils are able to pit themselves against the odds, often gaining at least the necessary minimum five GCSEs (*General Certificate of Secondary Education*) followed by two good A-levels (*Advanced levels*) which gives them the possibility of entrance into university. Others follow the more practically based GNVQ (*General National Vocational Qualification*) route to further education, which can also lead to degrees. The skills and talents of many dyslexic children are all too readily considered to be of secondary importance in the school curriculum. These skills may include business acumen, design, jewellery-making, pottery and so forth. Academic subjects tend to be rated more highly because they are the more usual subjects read at university. League tables may emphasise this too. But there is more to life than university education – people in all walks of life with all types of skills are of vital importance to a country's economy. Until educationalists give *equal value to all subjects* taught in school there will be a two-tier attitude to any system, with a tendency to value the academic above the practical. What stupid intellectual snobbery! The skills of each child should be nurtured, and his or her talents developed as fully as possible. Teachers need to acquire the knack of spotting the talents and interests of the children in their class – which many of them, of course, already do. Reassurance must be given that value as a human being is not dependent on, for example, results in a History exam! Once children appreciate how they personally can learn, their confidence in their ability and attitude to school can change dramatically.

The earlier the recognition of a child's dyslexia, the better. A reception class teacher is in a good position to notice which children are slow to start. If, as a matter of course, these children were given the appropriate physical exercises and taught with a multisensory approach, they would be less likely to think of themselves as failures. Fortunately, more and more children with learning difficulties are now having exercises at school – sometimes as a club – with very beneficial results in their ability to learn.

If a dyslexic child is not given help for his learning difficulties in his junior years, time begins to run out and he will not have the literacy skills to cope with the GCSE curriculum and all its requirements. More dyslexic children these days are being recognised at an early age and receive specialist tuition in their junior schools. This gives a good chance of their reading and spelling being adequate when they are about 11 years old. At that point remedial help may be terminated. But as the educational demands increase, especially during the GCSE syllabus, it is important that appropriate support is available as and when needed.

A child's problems either with communication or organisation – both are difficult for others to live with – need specific attention in the same way as do reading and spelling difficulties. *Good self-esteem is vital for success*. Any child who feels worthless may either withdraw or become defiant of the system and develop behavioural problems of some sort. Many take to truancy because time spent in school seems pointless, and later in life their poor literacy is often put down to their playing truant. But do small children really play truant at the age at which they are being taught to read and write? Or is it not, rather, at a later age, when methods have been used that failed to strike the learning chord, and re-applied only to reinforce the failure, that truancy begins in earnest? It seems that the watershed occurs around the age of 11 when a severely dyslexic child has already experienced five to six years of failure. Prior to that, especially in the 5–7-year-old period, children are usually eager to learn and keen to please and compete on equal terms with their peers. Disillusionment and feelings of inadequacy can change all that!

If children are written off – even implied to be stupid or lazy – they will be inclined to give up and then leave school with no particular skills that they can market in order to provide them with work. They will tend to feel worthless, angry and aggressive and let down by the system. They may even get into trouble and end up in prison. The prison population has a very high percentage of illiteracy. What a dreadful thing if our education system has done this to them! Also, it is such a loss to society of potential talent, not to mention the financial outlay of the taxpayer which could be put to so much better and more positive use. This is an appalling state of affairs. Tragically, it is not unknown for a child at school to feel so desperate about his lack of success that he commits suicide.

Some teachers will be familiar with the Instrumental Enrichment Programme devised by Rueven Feuerstein. Most of Feuerstein's work in Israel has been directed towards children who have been through traumatic deprivations due to social and political upheavals in their countries. However, he too has appreciated the fact that children who cannot learn traditional factual information in schools can be taught to become independent thinkers and develop strategies to solve problems and be stimulated by discussion in the process. This type of observation and clear and logical thinking is the basis of Raven's Progressive Matrices which Feuerstein used to develop thinking skills. Thinking skills programmes, such as the Somerset Thinking Skills, are being introduced very successfully as part of the curriculum in many schools. All pupils benefit from learning how to evaluate tasks. They learn to divide tasks into manageable parts, focus on one part at a time, note relationships, follow a plan, use hypotheses and self-questioning, check responses, and recognise that there are different ways to reach a conclusion. Oral skills can be improved enormously as the interaction of the group teaches them how to discuss, compare, explain, and decide – changing opinions if necessary – and then draw conclusions.

It has been noted that these practices spill over positively into their work generally. It is also invaluable for those pupils who have experienced difficulty in self-organisation. There are instances of a dramatic improvement in reading as well.

Children should be learning to *see* rather than simply *look*, to *listen* rather than merely *hear*. The aim should be to present material in as many different ways as possible in order to stimulate and provide learning skills for all of them. A class teacher must look for a child's **strengths** in order to teach effectively. Such teaching would lessen the enormous numbers of children who are currently experiencing these difficulties.

Advances in computer technology may well lighten the load for the dyslexic child in the classroom and in further education. Developments in software have now made available programs where a child can record ideas and then have spelling and syntax corrected as he operates the keyboard. It is hoped that the financial outlay will decrease as it has with other technological equipment, resulting in widespread use.

There are people who advocate that their work provides a cure for dyslexia. Their methods may help a child to relax and build up confidence, but will not enable him to read and spell all words accurately. As has been said before, appropriate teaching is essential and *more time is always needed* – more time in the early days *to get letters sorted out* – then, more time *to write words down*; later, more time *to write essays* and more time *to do exams*. Extra time may be allowed in external examinations if it is applied for in an appropriate way. After leaving school, these young adults may still need more time *to gain job qualifications* and come into their own. They are often termed *late developers*.

Conclusions

Many teachers are realising that, as they find out more about dyslexia and, indeed, dyspraxia, attention deficit disorder, and speech and language processing problems, they are able to appreciate the puzzling or irritating behaviour in some children. Even the mere knowledge of the reasons changes the teacher's attitude from exasperation to understanding, and this positive approach will make a child's time at school more bearable and constructive.

By enabling children to experience the two aspects of special education – the movement exercises and the cognitive tuition – their lives at school could be transformed. If schools could be persuaded to adopt this joint approach, behaviour problems would diminish, and considerable expense could be saved by education authorities. But above all, these children would have a more satisfying time at school. They would then begin to thrive in an unexpected way and lead interesting and fulfilling lives.

Suggested further reading/ resources

Agnew, M., Barlow, S., Pascal, L. and Skidmore, S. (1995) *Get Better Grades*, London: Piccadilly Press.

Arbor, A. (1996) *Ann Arbor Tracking Programs*, Northumberland: Ann Arbor Publishers Ltd.

Aston Index, Learning Developmental Aids, Duke Street, Wisbech, Cambs. PE13 2AE.

Bangor Dyslexia Test, Cambs: LDA.

Bigland, S., Speake, J. and Thomas, J. (1992) *Cambridge Language Activity File*, Ponteland: STASS Publications.

Brand, V. (2002) *Spelling Made Easy*, Baldock: Egon Publishers.

—— (2002) *Remedial Spelling*, Baldock: Egon Publishers.

British Picture Vocabulary Scale, 2nd edn, Dunn, L.M. and Dunn, L.M. (1982) *BPVS*, NFER-Nelson.

Burge, V. (1986) *Dyslexia – Basic Numeracy*, Helen Arkell Dyslexia Centre, Frensham, Surrey, GU10 3BW.

Buzan, T. (2003) *Use Your Head*, revised edn, London: BBC Books.

—— (2003) *Use Your Memory*, revised edn, London: BBC Books.

—— with Buzan, B. (2003) *The Mind Map Book*, revised edn, London: BBC Books.

Chinn, S. (1996) *What to Do When You Can't Learn the Times Tables*, Baldock: Egon Publishers.

—— (2003) *Test of Thinking Style in Mathematics*, Mark: Markco Publishing.

—— (2004) *The Trouble with Maths*, London: RoutledgeFalmer.

—— and Ashcroft, R. (1998) *Dyslexia and Mathematics: A Teaching Handbook*, 2nd edn, London: Whurr.

Clay, M. (1995) *Reading Recovery – A Guidebook for Teachers in Training*, NZ: Heinemann.

Cognitive Abilities Test – CAT, 3rd edn, Windsor: NFER.

Cowdery, L., Morse, P. and Prince, M. (1985) *Teaching Reading Through Spelling*, Clwyd: TRTS Publications.

Cripps, C. (1998) *A Hand for Spelling*, LDA.

Crystal, D. (1988) *Rediscover Grammar*, London: Longman.

—— (1993) *Listen to your Child*, Harmondsworth: Penguin.

Davies, A. and Richie, D. (2003) *Teaching THRASS Whole-Picture Keyword Phonics: The Essential Guide to Progression and Assessment for all Teachers of English*, THRASS, www.thrass.co.uk.

Dennison, G.E. and Dennison, P.E. (1981) *Switching On – A Guide to Kinaesthetics,* California: Educational Kinaesthetics Inc.

Dennison, P. (1984) *Edu K for Kids,* California: Educational Kinaesthetics Inc.

Deterding, G. and Scheib, B. (1992) *Steps to Literacy,* Hitchin: Nisbet.

Dr Seuss Books (1960 onwards) New York: Random House Inc.

Dyslexia: Integrating Theory and Practice (1991) Proceedings of the 2nd British Dyslexia Association International Conference, Whurr.

Edith Norrie Letter Case (1971) Helen Arkell Dyslexia Centre, Frensham, Surrey, GU10 3BW.

Gardner, H. (1993) *Frames of Mind,* London: Fontana.

Gillingham, A. and Stillman, B. W. (1960) *Simultaneous Oral Spelling – SOS, The Gillingham Manual,* 8th edn, Educators Pub. Service.

Harris, M. and Coltheart, M. (1990) *Language Processing in Children and Adults,* London: Routledge.

Hartmann, T. (1993) *Attention Deficit Disorder: A Different Perception,* Grass Valley, CA: Underwood Books.

Henderson, A. (1998) *Maths for the Dyslexic: A Practical Guide,* London: David Fulton.

Hickey Multi-Sensory Language Course (2002) Helen Arkell Dyslexia Centre, Frensham, Surrey, GU10 3BW.

Hornsby, B. and Shear, F. (1993) *Alpha to Omega,* 4th edn, Oxford: Heinemann Educational Books.

Lloyd, S. and Wernham, S. (1995) *Jolly Phonics,* Chigwell: Jolly Learning.

McGuiness, C. and McGuiness, G. (1996) *Phono-Graphix,* Florida: Orton Annals of Dyslexia.

—— and —— (1998) *Reading Reflex,* London: Penguin.

Miles, T. and Gilroy, D. (1996) *Dyslexia at College,* 2nd edn, London: Methuen.

Miles, T. R. and Miles, E. (1999) *Dyslexia a Hundred Years On,* revised edn, Milton Keynes: Open University Press.

Montgomery, D. (1997) *Spelling – Remedial Strategies,* Special Needs in Ordinary Schools Series, London: Cassell.

Mosely, D. and Nicol, C. (1986) *Ace Spelling Dictionary,* Wisbech, Cambs: Learning Development Aids.

Mosley, J. (1996) *Quality Circle Time in the Primary Classroom,* Wisbech: LDA.

Naglieri, J. A. (1985) *MAT – Matrix Analogies Test,* USA: The Psychological Corporation Harcourt Brace Jovanovich.

Nash-Wortham, M. and Hunt, J. (2002) *Take Time,* 2nd edn, Stourbridge: The Robinswood Press.

National Curriculum (1995) Department for Education.

National Literacy Strategy (1998) DfEE – Department for Education and Employment.

Neale Analysis of Reading Ability (1989) Windsor: NFER.

Ostler, C. (1991) *Dyslexia – A Parents' Survival Guide,* Godalming: Ammonite Books.

—— (1996) *Study Skills – A Pupil's Survival Guide,* Godalming: Ammonite Books.

—— and Ward, F. (2001) *Advance Study Skills,* Wakefield: SEN Marketing.

Peer, L. and Reid, G. (2003) *Introduction to Dyslexia,* London: David Fulton.

Pheloung, B. (1986) *Help your Child to Learn,* Sydney, NSW: Tortoiseshell Press.

—— (1997) *Help Your Class to Learn*, Manley NSW: Barbara Pheloung.

Pollock, J. (1992) *Signposts to Spelling*, 3rd edn (Autumn 2004), Wakefield: SEN Marketing.

—— and Waller, E. (1999) *English Grammar and Teaching Strategies: Lifeline to Literacy*, London: David Fulton.

Portwood, M. (1996) *Developmental Dyspraxia*, London: David Fulton.

—— (2003) *Dyslexia and Physical Education*, London: David Fulton.

Pumphrey, P. and Reason, R. (1991) *Specific Learning Difficulty (Dyslexia)*, London: Routledge.

Raven's Progressive Matrices – NFER.

Rinaldi, W. (1992) *Social Use of Language Programme*, Windsor: NFER-Nelson.

Sharron, H. (1987) *Changing Children's Minds (Feuerstein's Revolution in the Teaching of Intelligence)*, Birmingham: Questions Publishing Co. Ltd.

Stirling, E. G. (1984) *Spelling Checklist*, 114 Westbourne Road, Sheffield S10 2QT.

—— (1985) *Help for the Dyslexic Adolescent*, 114 Westbourne Road, Sheffield S10 2QT.

Stordy, J. and Nicholl, M. (2002) *The Remarkable Nutritional Treatment for ADHD, Dyslexia and Dyspraxia*, London: Macmillan.

Teaching and Learning Spellings (1999) Helen Arkell Dyslexia Centre, Frensham, Surrey, GU10 3BW.

Thomson, M. E. (1989) *Developmental Dyslexia*, 3rd edn, London: Whurr.

Thomson, P. and Gilchrist, P. (eds) (1996) *Dyslexia: A Multidisciplinary Approach*, London: Chapman & Hall.

Weatherill, C. (2003) *Primary Playground Games*, Leamington Spa: Scholastic Ltd.

Wendon, L. (1984) *Letterland (The Pictogram System)*, Cambridge: Letterland Ltd, Barton CB3 7AY.

Westwood, P. (1993) *Commonsense Methods for Children with Special Needs*, 2nd edn, London: Routledge.

Wilson, J. (1997) *PAT – Phonological Awareness Training*, Educational Psychology Service, County Hall, Aylesbury, Bucks HP20 1UZ.

Wood, E. (1993) *Spelling Workbooks 1–3*, 3rd impression, London: Hodder & Stoughton.

Video/DVD/CD Roms

Coming Round to Circle Time: (video) Bristol: Lucky Duck Publications.

Movement to Learn: (video and DVD) Barbara Pheloung, Wakefield: SEN Marketing.

Wordshark, Numbershark: (PC) London: White Space.

Addresses

FURTHER INFORMATION FOR TEACHERS, STUDENTS AND PARENTS

United Kingdom

British Dyslexia Association, 98 London Road, Reading, Berks RG1 5AU
The British Dyslexia Association is the umbrella organisation from whom information can be obtained on local associations, courses for teachers, conferences, literature and computer programmes. Tel. 0118 966 8271

Helen Arkell Dyslexia Centre, Frensham, Farnham, Surrey GU10 3BW
Dyslexia Institute, Park House, Wick Road, Egham, Surrey TW20 0HH
Dyslexia Scotland, Stirling Business Centre, Wellgreen, Stirling FK8 2DZ
Dyslexia Teaching Centre, 23 Kensington Square, London W8 5HN
Dyslexia Unit, University College of Wales, Bangor, Gwynedd LL57 2DG
Dyspraxia Foundation, 8 West Alley, Hitchin, Herts SG5 1EG
Hornsby International Centre, Wye Street, London SW11 2HB
Institute of Optometry, 56 Newington Causeway, London SE1 6DS
LADDER (for ADD), PO Box 700, Wolverhampton WV3 7YY
National Association for Special Educational Needs (NASEN), York House, Exhall Grange, Wheelwright Lane, Coventry CV7 9HP
PATOSS (The Professional Association of Teachers and Students with Specific Learning Difficulties), PO Box 10, Evesham, Worcs WR11 1ZW. Tel. 01386 712650. Email patoss@evesham.ac.uk
Royal College of Speech and Language Therapists, 2/3 White Hart Yard, London SE1 1NX. Tel: 020 7378 1200

Ireland

Association for Children and Adults with Learning Disabilities, Suffolk Chambers, 1 Suffolk Street, Dublin 2

Europe

European Dyslexia Association, Av. Charles Woeste 38 Bt. 7, 1090
Brussels, Belgium

United States

Association for Children with Learning Difficulties, 5225 Grace Street,
Pittsburgh, PA 15236
Orton Society, Chester Building, Suite 382, 8600 La Salle Road, Baltimore,
MD 21204

Australia

SPELD NSW, 7 Acron Street, St Ives, NSW 2075
SPELD WA, Box 409, South Perth, WA 6951
SPELD Victoria, 494 Brunswick Street, North Fitzroy, Victoria 3065

New Zealand

SPELD, PO Box 27112, Wellington
Seabrook McKenzie Centre, 15 Rastrick Street, Christchurch 1

Canada

Canadian Association for Children with Learning Difficulties, Maison
Kildare House, 323 Chapel Street, Suite 200, Ottawa KIN 272

South Africa

SAALED, Association for Learning and Education, PO Box 2404,
Clareinch 7740, Cape Town

PUBLISHERS AND SUPPLIERS OF BOOKS AND TEACHING MATERIALS FOR DYSLEXIC PUPILS

Ann Arbor Publishers, PO Box 1, Belford, Northumberland NE70 7JK
Better Books, 3 Paganel Drive, Dudley, West Midlands DY1 4AZ
Crossbow Games, 41 Sawpit Lane, Brocton, Stafford ST17 0TE
Gamz, 25 Albert Park Road, Malvern, Worcestershire WR14 1HW
Helen Arkell Dyslexia Centre, Frensham, Farnham, Surrey GU10 3BW
Learning Development Aids (LDA), Duke Street, Wisbech, Cambs PE13
2AE

Learning Materials Ltd, Dixon Street, Wolverhampton WV2 2BX

Letterland Ltd, Barton, Cambridge CB2 7AY

SEN Marketing, 18 Leeds Road, Outwood, Wakefield WF1 2LT. Tel: 01924 871 697

Softease Ltd, Market Place, Ashbourne, Derbyshire DE6 1ES

Special Educational Needs, 9 The Close, Church Aston, Newport, Shropshire TF10 9JL

Swallow Systems, PIP (Pixie), 134 Cock Lane, High Wycombe, Bucks HP13 7EA

Whurr Publishers Ltd, 19b Compton Terrace, London N1 2UN

Index

Main entries in bold type